To

Kathy McILNutt

From

Robin Dean
With Love

Date

March 2011

A BEAUTIFUL LIFE

A BEAUTIFUL LIFE

DEVOTIONS FOR A WOMAN'S HEART

by Gwen Ford Faulkenberry

summerside
PRESS

Stories written by other authors are as follows: "Obedience" and "Devotion" by René Schay Ford; quotations in "Fullness" have been taken from the book *Only a Clay Vessel, The Story of Leota Campbell*, by Irene B. Brand. Copyright, 1985; "Love" by Desirée Beck Beard; "Light" by Charlene Solum Lessin.

Cover design by Loveseat Creative. Interior layout by James Baker Design.

Published by Summerside Press, Inc., 11024 Quebec Circle, Bloomington, Minnesota 55438 | www.summersidepress.com

Summerside Press™ is an inspirational publisher offering fresh, irresistible books to uplift the heart and delight the mind.

Printed in China.

For Grace, Adelaide, Madeline, and Sophia,
and daughters of the King everywhere.

The king is enthralled by your beauty;
honor him, for he is your lord.

Psalm 45:11 NIV

Mirror I am seeing a new reflection
I'm looking into the eyes
Of [Him] who made me and to Him
I have beauty beyond compare
I know He defines me…

"Mirror"
Barlow Girl, 2004

Her full nature spent itself in deeds which left no great name on the earth, but the effect of her being on those around her was incalculable; for the growing good of the world is partly dependent on unhistoric acts, and on all those…who live faithfully their hidden lives and rest in unvisited tombs.

—George Eliot
Middlemarch TV screenplay,
© 1994 British Broadcasting Corporation

Contents

A Beautiful Life Is…

A BEAUTIFUL LIFE

...Is a Life of the Spirit

Your beauty should come from within you—the beauty...
that will never be destroyed and is very precious to God.
1 PETER 3:4 NCV

---

s women, we are bombarded with many definitions of beauty. In popular culture as well as many Christian circles, it seems that beauty is sometimes defined by ideals we may either choose to reject outright or aspire to—but are never able to reach. Neither of these options is edifying for a real woman.

This book's focus is God's definition of beauty and, specifically, what it means to live a beautiful life before Him. If we, as women, take seriously the directive offered in 1 Peter 3:4, which says, "Your beauty should come from within you," then it seems worth exploring just what real beauty is. Or what it can be.

First and foremost, a beautiful life is a life of the Spirit. The verse above is quoted from the New Century Version, which is easy to understand, but I also like how the King James puts it: "Let [your beauty] be the hidden man of the heart, in that which is not corruptible." That concept of the "hidden man of the heart" speaks to me. And what woman isn't looking for beauty that lasts—i.e., is "not corruptible"?

The hidden man of the heart—our hope for lasting beauty—is the Holy Spirit of God. It is by Him, through

Him, and in Him that our hearts and therefore our lives can be transformed into something eternally, breathtakingly beautiful.

What exactly does that mean, though? And how do we find it? I believe Christian women can almost become as confused about the issue of beauty by sitting in some churches today—or by Christian media—as we do when we look at the world. Inner beauty, a beauty that lasts, a life lived in the Spirit—those things all sound good. But for some of us, these ideas seem just as unattainable as a size-four body or the perfect color of hair. We may decide to approach them like we do a job or a course of study—as something to work for, to achieve excellence in through personal ambition.

A life of the Spirit isn't some huge thing that happens to us all at once.

My friend Char tells a story about how she began to live a life of the Spirit. She was in Bible college, and at her school, you had to work to pay for your tuition. One day at her job the boss, who was also one of her professors, asked the group not to visit while they were working. He left the room, and they proceeded to talk.

That evening, Char felt convicted that she had been wrong to disobey her boss by talking while he was gone. She decided to find him and apologize. Expecting to be reprimanded for her misconduct, Char was very surprised when the professor looked at her and smiled. "I'm glad you've learned to listen to the voice of the Holy Spirit," he told her. And that was it.

In many ways, that *is* it. A life of the Spirit isn't some huge thing that happens to us all at once. We can't get a "spiritual makeover" or earn a Bible degree that suddenly makes us beautiful in the Spirit. It's an inner work of God that takes place when we say yes to His leading, moment by moment, one day at a time.

Prayer and Reflection:

Lord, I want to say yes to Your leading today, in every moment. I invite You to work in my heart and transform my life into something beautiful.

A BEAUTIFUL LIFE

...Is a Life of His Presence

"I am God Almighty. Live in My presence."
GENESIS 17:1 HCSB

The idea for this book came to me shortly after I moved into my new house. My parents had given us land overlooking the Arkansas River, and my husband and I had saved our money for years, looking forward to the moment when we could build our dream home and raise our growing family. After renting, scrimping, working, and planning, finally that moment had come. We had survived the building phase and the moving in—and, finally, we were home.

It was fall, and I'd just finished unpacking the last box. The lights in the cabinets were shimmering, the wood floor was freshly polished, and I was sitting on my couch admiring the natural stone of the fireplace in front of me and the oak mantel I designed. It was a Martha Stewart moment! Taking a sip of hot chocolate, I looked out the window at our deck and the majestic Arkansas River flowing far beneath me, carving its way through the Ozark Mountains bursting with color. A feeling of satisfaction flooded my soul. It's true what the Bible says: "Hope deferred makes the heart sick, but a longing fulfilled is a tree of life" (Proverbs 13:12 NIV).

I closed my eyes, breathing in the sweetness of that fulfillment and thanking the Lord for making our dream come true. My heart was filled to the brim with joy. And there in the stillness of my living room, I felt Him speak softly to my heart.

It was not an audible voice, but His meaning was very clear: *"This home is a place for you to live a beautiful life before Me. I have freely given it to you to enjoy, but you must always remember that* the beauty of your life and home has nothing to do with what you can see. It is My presence—and My presence alone—that makes something beautiful."

The beauty of your life and home has nothing to do with what you can see.

I've seen that principle operate over and over in my life and home. After several years, the wood floor is no longer freshly polished, and most days it desperately needs to be swept. The mantel usually wants to be dusted, and the deck is littered with my children's toys. My house is a lot like my body, I suppose—it doesn't always get the care it requires in order to look its best. But it's a beautiful place. Whether we're hosting a group of friends, bowing our heads at the dinner table, or tucking our kids into bed—Jesus is here. And His presence makes all of the difference.

Jesus, it is You I'm craving. I need Your presence. Without You, nothing matters. But with You beside me, every moment can be beautiful—even the difficult ones—because You are beautiful.

A BEAUTIFUL LIFE

...Is a Life of Abandon

And there was a woman in the city who was a sinner; and when she learned that [Jesus] was reclining at the table in the Pharisee's house, she brought an alabaster vial of perfume, and standing behind Him at His feet, weeping, she began to wet His feet with her tears, and kept wiping them with the hair of her head, and kissing His feet and anointing them with the perfume.

LUKE 7:37–38 NASB

We don't even know the woman's name. Some commentators have suggested that she was Mary, the sister of Martha, or Mary Magdalene. She could have been a prostitute or some other miserable representative of the female gender who had broken God's law. An outcast in Jewish society. Luke just tells us that she was a *sinner*.

I can see her there on the dusty street of Jerusalem. Perhaps she first saw Jesus teaching on the steps of the temple. Maybe she hid and watched at a distance as He picked up children and held them on His lap. Or maybe she talked to the woman with the issue of blood who had touched the hem of His garment and was instantly made whole.

However the woman—this sinner—was associated with Jesus, one thing is clear. She didn't just know *about* Him. In fact, in the midst of this dinner party at a religious leader's house, it appears she was the only one who really knew Him—the one who understood Him best.

The Bible says that when Jesus entered Simon's house, no one washed His feet. No one kissed Him or anointed His head with oil. But this lady, who was not invited to the party, showed up and threw herself at Jesus' feet, kissing them and weeping her heart out. She poured expensive ointment—presumably all she had—and wiped His feet with her hair. It was an act of both honor and total trust.

I must honor His holiness, and I must trust Him not to turn me away.

This behavior was shocking to others at the table. *If only Jesus knew what a sinner she was*, Simon thought to himself, *He wouldn't let her carry on so. He certainly wouldn't let her touch Him. He must not be a prophet after all!*

Even as Simon was musing on these things, Jesus, who was so much more than a prophet, read his thoughts. He tells a story about a creditor who forgives two debts, one large and one small. "Which one do you think loved him the most, Simon?" Jesus asked him. And the answer was obvious: *The one who owed the most*. Jesus went on to compare the woman to that person who owed a lot of money. He said, "Her sins, which are many, have been forgiven, for she loved much" (Luke 7:47 NASB).

There are lots of important lessons in this story, but the

thing that challenges me most is Jesus' description of the woman in that last sentence: "*She loved much.*"

It seems safe to say that the woman was recklessly abandoned in her love for Jesus. She wasn't invited to the party; she made a fool of herself by showing up. But she couldn't stay away. The perfume was expensive, far too extravagant to use on someone's feet. But she poured it out on Jesus anyway. Simon—and no doubt his Pharisee friends—judged her harshly. She had to have known they would. But she didn't care. She didn't care about anything or anyone else in that moment but Jesus.

Wow. Am I that caught up in His majesty, His beauty, that I'll make a fool of myself to express my love for Him? It's even hard for me sometimes to lift my hands in praise. After all, I go to a pretty conservative church. What might some people think?

Or what about the academic setting in which I teach? Jesus is not that popular among a lot of intellectuals. At least not the Jesus who claimed He was the only way to God. If I say how much I love Him, they may all think I'm stupid. I'd better hold back.

However, as I read the story of this woman who bathed Jesus' feet with her perfume and tears, wiping them off with her hair, I want that kind of reckless abandon. I want to be like her, to love Him like crazy and cling to His feet, regardless of what anyone else thinks. And to do that, I have to stay aware of my need.

The key to this woman's love for Jesus seems clear by her description. She was, indeed, a sinner. She was desperately in need of a Savior—and desperately aware of it. In her need she was not so different from me or you or even the Pharisees.

But what about her awareness? This woman was so aware of what she was that she was willing to do anything to have His forgiveness, His love, His peace. She was so undone by His amazing glory that she bowed down at His feet.

I'm afraid, in my pride, there are times I'm more like a Pharisee—blind to how needy I am. Once in a while, in severe mercy, the Lord pulls back the curtain and shows me just how ugly my heart can be. It's scary. In those moments, nothing else matters but Him. There's no other option but to fall at His feet, to throw myself on the altar of His love. I must honor His holiness, and I must trust Him not to turn me away.

I believe that's the message of this woman's life, and that's where I want to stay.

Prayer and Reflection:

My dear Jesus, thank You that You never turn me away. I'm casting myself—all of my hopes and dreams, all of my failures and regrets, everything—at Your feet today. I bow my face before Your glory. I pour out my life before Your mercy. Receive my love and honor, Holy One. Take this empty vessel and fill it with Your beauty.

A BEAUTIFUL LIFE

...Is a Life of Submission

Father...not My will, but [always] Yours be done.
LUKE 22:42 AMP

───────────────────────

I am the mother of a very gifted child who also fits the textbook definition of "strong willed." This will is something I celebrate most of the time. I enjoy her spunk, admire her passion, and delight in her fierce loyalty and determination. I recognize the value of her strength and know that if it is properly bent—not broken—it can be a beautiful thing. I dwell in these lovely possibilities most of the time. The rest of the time I am either praying or pulling out my hair. Or both.

Yesterday was a hair-pulling day. My daughter asked me for something she wanted. It was a simple request and, I'm sure, seemed to her a very good thing. To her it was not much to ask, and I could have easily said yes. But, as her mother, I could see that it wasn't the best thing, and the answer I gave her was *no*.

A fit ensued. There was kicking and screaming and much gnashing of teeth, which had to be dealt with accordingly. After peace was restored, there was opportunity for discussion.

In my great wisdom I explained that happy obedience takes a lot of trust. "You obeyed me," I said, "but only after I disciplined you. All of the crying and resisting caused you misery and wasted precious moments of our lives. Wouldn't it have been better to cheerfully accept the answer I gave you, even if it wasn't what you wanted to hear?"

"But I wanted you to say yes," she replied. "I really wanted that, and I didn't understand why you said *no*."

I told her, "You have to trust me that I know what is best, even when you don't understand. I am your mommy, and that is one of my jobs—to know what you need and to give it to you. When I say no it's because I can see that what you want is not what you need."

Sometimes His greatest mercies are His refusals.

This was all hard for my young daughter to digest. She wanted her own way.

"Grace," I said, feeling the irony of her name for the millionth time, "do you know that I love you very, very much?"

"Yes."

"Can you trust me to do the thing I believe is best for you—the thing that will bring about the most good in your life—because of how much I love you?"

A pause. "Yes."

"You need to think about that when you ask me for something. Then, if I say *no*, you can be just as happy as if I said yes, because you know I will only do what I believe is good for you."

She eyed me warily. Then, finally, she accepted what I was saying as the truth.

I pray that the concept, as a tiny seed, takes root somewhere in her little heart. It's a lesson she'll refer to again and again, as I was reminded that night in my prayers—another strong-willed child presenting her requests.

"Father, I really want this and this and this and this to happen. Can I have those things, Lord? You, who have infinite wisdom, can surely see how wonderful it would be. And with inexhaustible resources, You can bring it to pass, can't You, Lord? Will You? Soon?"

"I certainly can, and I may. That's for Me to decide. But what if My answer is *no*? What then? Can you trust Me, as you advised your daughter? Do you really believe that I know best?" came the still, small voice.

Humbled, I had no alternative but to practice what I had preached. I had to lay down my will before *His* perfect will and trust His love.

Elisabeth Elliot writes that "sometimes His greatest mercies are His refusals." I don't like hearing that any more than my daughter likes hearing *no*. But it's the truth. He knows best. And the happy, obedient child of God trusts in His love however He chooses to answer our questions.

An old hymn puts it this way: "Trust and obey, for there's no other way, to be happy in Jesus—but to trust and obey!"

Prayer and Reflection:

Father, I choose to trust You today. You know best. Help me to keep my heart at rest in the wisdom of Your will, Your way, and Your timing.

A BEAUTIFUL LIFE

...Is a Life of Obedience

*And do not seek what you should eat or what you should drink, nor
have an anxious mind. For all these things the nations of the world
seek after, and your Father knows that you need these things. But
seek the kingdom of God, and all these things shall be added to you.*
LUKE 12:29–31 NKJV

Carly knew she needed to make a cake for a dear friend
who had lost her husband not long ago. She got out all the
ingredients for her famous homemade chocolate cake and
icing and started mixing, spooning, and baking. In the middle
of all of this, however, Carly felt the Lord say, "Make another
chocolate cake."

"What? Lord, I feel like You are telling me to make another
chocolate cake...." Carly could not audibly hear the Lord speak,
but she knew that He was speaking nonetheless. Not only was
she supposed to make another chocolate cake, it was supposed
to be put into a disposable pan. So Carly went to work on
another cake and baked it in a disposable pan. She felt a little
crazy but obeyed anyway.

She started to make her famous chocolate icing when the
voice stopped her and said, "No nuts."

"No nuts! I always put nuts in my icing. Are You sure I am
supposed to leave them out?"

"No nuts."

Though it pained her to do so, Carly made the icing without nuts. Before long, she had two beautiful chocolate cakes on her counter. She knew where one was going. And she believed that before the day was through, the other one would find a home, too. So she waited.

In just a little while, her doorbell rang. She had been expecting someone from church to come over to help her with her computer. When she opened the door, her jaw dropped. Her friend, Ted, did not look like himself at all. In fact, he closely resembled a chipmunk hoarding nuts for the winter.

He is... meeting all of your needs right down to the finest details.

"Ted, what happened to you?" Carly asked.

He explained as best he could through the gauze in the cheeks that he had all of his wisdom teeth taken out, his wife was out of town, and he was sick of slurping soup. He went on to ask, "Is that chocolate cake I smell?"

Carly smiled and asked, "Could you eat chocolate cake if it didn't have any nuts in it?"

Ted, with a look of fierce excitement in his eyes, said, "Yes, Mrs. Carly, I sure could."

"Well then, Ted, I made you a cake today."

Isn't it amazing that the God of the universe cares so much for us that He wants us to have chocolate cake? Ted did not have to have chocolate cake to live. He could have made it just fine without it, but it was important to the Lord that he had not just a piece of cake but the whole thing.

The Lord cared so much about Ted that He prompted Carly to bake an extra cake that morning. And because she listened and obeyed, Carly got to participate in an extra-sweet blessing. The Lord was in her kitchen just like He is with you right now—in your favorite chair, in the car as you're riding along, anywhere you are—He is there. And He is watching you, speaking to you, loving you, and meeting all of your needs right down to the finest details. What a beautiful example of obedience, the story of Carly and her cake. But more importantly, what an awesome God!

Prayer and Reflection:

Father, I thank You that You care about my life down to the tiniest detail. Thank You for how You provide for all of my needs. As I walk through this day, I want to be obedient to You. Speak to me, Father, as I listen for Your voice, and give me the courage to obey You.

A BEAUTIFUL LIFE

...Is a Life of Letting Go

Love goes on forever.
1 CORINTHIANS 13:8 TLB

'Ve just had one of the worst weeks I can remember, and though I can point to several different factors that contributed to my emotional demise (my house was a mess, I had a fender-bender, I failed again at my attempt to eat right and exercise, and I didn't get any writing done), the central glaring cause of my horrible week was that my son, Harper, started kindergarten.

I wasn't ready, to say the least. Although well-meaning people had told me it would be easier this time, I knew in my heart that it wouldn't. Two years ago, amid my lamentations over my oldest daughter starting school, I heard things like, "The first time is always the worst. Next time it won't bother you this bad." And my favorite, "At least you still have Harper."

Now, I know some of you are thinking, *What's the big deal?* For many people it's not a life change when their kids go to school; they've been going to preschool for years. Some moms, even stay-at-home moms, are glad when their children go to school. They celebrate the new opportunities and exciting experiences their children—and they—will have. It's considered a healthy, natural part of life, and I respect that. They're probably the sane ones. Only I'm not one of those moms. It feels so *unnatural* to me.

While I enjoy my work and have plenty of goals I want to accomplish that aren't directly related to child-rearing, there's this strong attachment I feel to home and having my kids there. It goes beyond visceral. It's animal. I'm a mother hen, and I like all of my chicks under my wings, even if they get in the way when I'm trying to type a manuscript.

The Lord is doing a new thing, and it's my job to embrace it.

Monday morning was a morning I'll never forget. I'd carefully ironed Harper's clothes the night before, and we'd checked his backpack for the fifteenth time, making sure that everything was ready. When he got dressed that morning, he bounded into my room to show me just how fast he could run in his shiny new shoes. "Do you think my teacher will like me?" he asked as I combed his wheat-colored hair. His eyes shone like big blue diamonds. I hugged him to me tight and said, "I know she will!" And I was hoping she'd *love* him. We both desperately needed her to.

When my husband and I walked him to his room at County Line Elementary School, there was a bulletin board outside that said WELCOME. It had all of the kids' names on bones and featured Clifford the Big Red Dog. Harper turned to me in sheer delight. How did she know Clifford was his favorite? "That must be a sign from God," I told him. He had to be the cutest kindergartner on the planet.

Mrs. Vernon, the teacher, greeted him with a hug, and they struck up a conversation about his birthday: "I noticed on your information sheet that your birthday is the same day as my daughter's—October 25!" Her eyes were warm and genuine, and her smile seemed to wrap Harper in a blanket of safety. I saw his confidence rising, the fun beginning, and I knew it was time for me to bow out.

Stone and I said little on the drive home. Before he left for work, we offered a prayer for Grace and Harper and asked God's blessings on their new year at school. I held back the dam when Stone hugged me good-bye…but when the door closed behind him, I sat down in my quiet house and cried.

Adelaide, my baby, was at my sister-in-law's house, and I had planned to work that day on this book. But every word I typed seemed to lead me back to Harper and Grace and what was once a beautiful life but was gone. I heard their footsteps on the floor behind me and saw their shadows playing in the yard. Ghosts that looked like them curled up in the recliner, reading *Frog and Toad Are Friends*, and others chased lizards down the sidewalk, catching one and bringing it to show me.

A black veil fell over my day. Instead of writing, I mourned. I mourned the changes that had happened and the changes yet to come. I mourned their littleness and how fast it had seemed to slip through my fingers. Had I cherished them enough? Loved them enough? Showed it enough? Prepared them enough? I hoped so, because those days of being home—all those hours that are strung together like pearls of a beautiful necklace—they're gone. That necklace is complete. That story ended.

It's taking me awhile to adjust to the next story, the one that's just beginning. I know there's so much to look forward to, and the shining look on Harper's face when he tells me about his day and his new friends and all he's learning—it compels me. Urges me on in this new direction. At the Spirit's coaxing, I peeked out from behind the veil this week. The Lord is doing a new thing, and it's my job to embrace it.

One thing I'll take away from this experience is the reminder that life is a vapor. For a short time our kids are small, our spouse is young, our parents are healthy—and all this if we're very blessed. But nothing here on earth lasts forever. Nothing, that is, except the love we put into those days, those hours that get strung together like pearls of a necklace. I want mine to be full of it.

PRAYER AND REFLECTION:

Lord, I don't like letting go. It's hard. But I believe it is Your way and so necessary to peace. By Your power at work within me, I choose to let go today and trust You.

A BEAUTIFUL LIFE

...Is a Life of Freedom

"The Spirit of the Lord GOD is upon Me, because the LORD has anointed Me to preach good tidings to the poor; He has sent Me to heal the brokenhearted, to proclaim liberty to the captives, and the opening of the prison to those who are bound."

ISAIAH 61:1 NKJV

Growing up in the same town, I knew who Dena was. Our families went way back, and her younger sister, Beth, was a friend of mine in high school. We both played the French horn in the band.

Beth idolized Dena, as younger sisters tend to do. Through her I heard how successful Dena was in everything, how smart, how wildly popular. Occasionally Beth would wear one of Dena's college sweatshirts to school, a gray one with big Greek letters on the front. That sweatshirt seemed sacred to her—like a mantle of greatness.

Beth didn't talk much about the wreck that happened several years before, when Dena was in high school and we were mere grade-schoolers. I knew about it, of course; everyone in town did. But the details were sketchy in my mind. I was too young to understand.

When I graduated from high school, Beth was a junior. Dena was in another state, on her way to becoming a successful lawyer.

I didn't see either one of them again until I moved back to my hometown and opened a café. By this time Dena had moved home, too, and one day she called to book a dinner. She was with a group of attorneys in the area who provided pro-bono advocacy for children and other free legal services to low-income families.

Judgment is bondage, whether we're judging ourselves or others.

Dena's easy manner, quick wit, and relaxed leadership style were all things that impressed me as I served the lawyers' cheese soup and chicken salads. For all of her intelligence, she seemed to exude a generosity of spirit that was guileless, as innocent as some of the people her group tried to protect. I thought she was a person I'd like to get to know.

Fast-forward to a couple of years later. I was a stay-at-home mom in search of some interesting friends, and I knew that Dena was staying home with her kids, too. I called her up out of the blue, and we decided to get together for a play date at her house the next week. It didn't take many of these meetings to bring us to the point of sharing the deep things of our hearts.

One day as we played with our girls among Barbies, face paint, and Usborne books, I asked Dena to tell me about the accident. Her big eyes instantly welled up with tears. "Some friends and I were out partying, and I was driving. I lost control of the car, and one of my best friends was killed."

The pain on her face showed me the magnitude of the wound, and a part of me felt sorry for opening it up. But another part knew—and knows from experience—that this opening up of ourselves can be a part of our healing.

She went on to tell me how the experience had changed her life forever. How kind the parents of her dead friend had been. "They never treated me badly or like they blamed me, but I have often blamed myself."

In the years that followed the tragedy, Dena tried to hide her free spirit under a cloak of grief that she pulled tight around her life, sometimes searching for ways to become a better Christian. In her guilt and confusion, she began to define herself—and others—by rules of behavior. Like so many of us, she thought she could make herself good and acceptable to God by refraining from certain activities. And she admits that she began to judge others by that same harsh standard. This way of life marked her next years with a spirit of heaviness.

"One evening," Dena said, "my eyes were opened to the futility of judgment. I was in college and visiting the apartment of a new friend. There were others there—people whose character I might have questioned. I didn't know them, but I was sure that some of them didn't fit the benchmark I thought I was supposed to uphold." Her eyes teared up again. "There was a moment when a girl I previously would have judged came to the door and flung it wide open. 'It's snowing!' she said, with the purity of a child."

Dena tilted her head and steadied her eyes at me, wiping away more tears. "I could feel in that moment, in that simple act, a spirit of goodness and kindness flood my heart. And for whatever things I had yet to learn of God and His ways, I felt the barriers I'd built crumble as these people interacted and accepted me with such grace.

"Judgment is bondage, whether we're judging ourselves or others. I set up those standards to try to atone for myself, to gain back something I'd lost when I had that wreck. But after I stepped into the wonder of the snowfall that evening, I realized that spiritual freedom is not something we attain by reaching standards we have set for ourselves. I also realized that I cannot place my standards upon others. Being delivered from judgment freed my heart to know something of God's true, inner beauty."

The burden of judgment Dena had carried since the accident fell from her shoulders that day, and she is vigilant in her efforts to avoid picking it back up. Though she will always regret what happened in that horrible wreck, she believes that the Lord has released her from judgment. And from the bondage of judging others.

"I'm not always successful, but I try to extend to others the unconditional love I feel I've received—regardless of the circumstances," Dena says.

These are words of beauty to my ears. A song of freedom, flowing from a liberated heart.

Prayer and Reflection:

Father, set me free from judging myself and judging others. Please help me to be able to receive the love You offer me, to comprehend how wide and deep it is. Transform me with Your love so that I can extend it to others.

A BEAUTIFUL LIFE

...Is a Life of Trust

Trust in the LORD with all your heart;
do not depend on your own understanding.
PROVERBS 3:5 NLT

*C*arrie Oliver is one of my heroes. At age forty-six, she was a devoted wife and mother of three boys, a Christian counselor, a well-known speaker, and an author. By anyone's definition this blond-haired, green-eyed runner was living a beautiful life.

Then, on May 17, 2005, Carrie received the news that she had pancreatic cancer. This diagnosis alone is grim, but worse still was the fact that Carrie's tumor was inoperable and the cancer had already spread to a lymph node in her neck. Her response is recorded in her journal:

Trauma, tragedy, and crisis. Certainly in my experience of being a human I felt these things, but what I know to be true… is that there was a moment where I came face-to-face with my Lord Jesus Christ and we talked about my choices, and really there were only two. One choice would be to succumb to the trauma and tragedy of it all and sink into a deep, dark, angry, depressed state and perhaps give up and give in to the statistics of the cancer that was growing in my body. The other choice…was to "choose" to cling tightly to Jesus and to "live" desperately, needing Him twenty-four hours a day and trusting that He would be there for me just as His scriptures have promised for thousands of years.

Against the odds, Carrie fought through two years of grueling chemo, radiation, and experimental treatments. Her life during those years seems to testify to what Paul wrote in 2 Corinthians 4:16: "Though outwardly we are wasting away, yet inwardly we are being renewed day by day" (NIV).

One of the hardest endeavors for humankind is to trust.

Here is a sampling of how she documented her journey:

June 14, 2005—This was going to be a whole new faith walk. My sovereign Lord has allowed this, and He has also been at work manifesting Himself to me…. God is still using me. I have a purpose every day that I awaken for every moment that I am still on this earth.

June 26, 2005—What do you do with all of this?… You trust. One of the hardest endeavors of humankind is to trust. To really trust that God is at work in my life in the way that He so chooses, in this here and for now.

August 7, 2005—The "what-ifs" start screaming at me. It is at that moment I straighten out my eyes on my path I am following and recount the verses such as Mark 11:22–25 and James 5. When I cry out to the Lord, He reminds me that I must not doubt His love and

*care and involvement in my life and He is healing me. Healing my
sin, my fears, my doubts, my selfishness, my pride, and He is at work
in my physical body, as well. Is this easy? Nope! Is it the best choice?
Yes! We have choices every day. I choose my God and His promises. I
choose to remember Psalm 91 and His promise that His angels are
holding me in His hands.*

*May 15, 2006—I celebrate finding Jesus to be all that He says He
is and trusting Him to strengthen me in my loneliest of moments
and to believe that His love is really all I ever need, even while
living on this earth…. This anniversary is a "marker" of God's
tremendous love.*

*September 22, 2006—It takes courage to fight the battle…. I am
a woman that in her humanness is very afraid, is sick, is weak, and
has no courage or strength. In my Lord Jesus Christ I am a woman
whose name means "Strong," I have faith, a sense of what I am
fighting for, and I have His arms to carry me.*

*November 13, 2006—I am glad that His promises are true and
that ultimately I can trust my Lord for everything this world has to
offer me, both wonderful and difficult.*

*June 13, 2007—I feel very confined at times. There are very few
things right now that I can do that I used to be able to do…. In
confinement we can focus in on or feel the immobility, Sorge says,
or we can experience the glorious intimacy of being held so firmly
in the Lord's arms. I have to go with the arms of the Lord…. Jesus,
I know that You love me, Jesus, I know that You love me, Jesus, I*

know that You love me and…Jesus, I love You, for You still have not left me or forsaken me. [I] am learning in the arms of Jesus [that] there is safety, there is intimacy, and there is something this world can never offer.

That was her last entry; Carrie died a few days later.

In this book we're exploring God's standard for a beautiful life. Once again, it's not the outward things that define us, or defined Carrie Oliver, but the hidden person of the heart. She had the incorruptible beauty of a heart that trusts. Not even cancer could destroy it. It's the kind of beauty that lives on forever.

For more of Carrie's story, visit www.carrieshealth.com.

PRAYER AND REFLECTION:

Jesus, thank You that I can find safety in Your arms from anything that assails me. Help me, Lord, to trust You no matter what, to find my strength and my joy in You alone. I want to have the kind of faith in You that no person or circumstance can shake.

A BEAUTIFUL LIFE

...*Is a Life of Belief*

For we walk by faith, not by sight.
2 CORINTHIANS 5:7 KJV

For me, life on earth is full of the abundance Jesus speaks of in John 10:10, when He says He came that we might have life and "have it more abundantly" (KJV). I live in a beautiful country setting, in a peaceful hamlet called Ozark on the Arkansas River. I have a wonderful husband, precious children, my extended family all around me, and I love my job. At times, the kingdom of heaven is so near that I can almost see it, touch it, feel it. And yet, this is not one of those times.

This week, the small town where I live has been touched by two major tragedies. The suicide of a school leader and the reported rape of a former "Miss OHS" in her new home in Mississippi has left everyone reeling. People are asking "Why?" Families are grieving. Churches are praying. I am lying awake at night pondering the mystery of suffering.

Both times this week I was informed of the news by a phone call. A strange thing happened as I listened to the people who told me each heartbreaking story. Of course I felt sad and also shocked. But the more I listened, the more I also felt anger rising up—at the enemy. His breath seemed so near that I could almost smell it, taste it, feel it. He was glad to hear the bad news. His is the kingdom of this earth.

As evil has once more surfaced in my personal version of Eden, I have been reminded that no matter how good life is at times here, this world is not our home. And I have been challenged to walk according to the laws of a different country. We can believe our circumstances or the climate of our surroundings, which can quickly change as mine did this week. Or we can believe God, choosing, instead of the natural reality we can see, the spiritual reality that is in Jesus. We can cling to eternal truths no matter what wind is blowing through the kingdom of this world.

We can cling to eternal truths no matter what wind is blowing through the kingdom of this world.

"Peace always—in all things," advises Amy Carmichael. I must lift up my eyes above the kingdom of this world and find my help in the Lord. Peace is possible in all things for those who walk in faith.

Prayer and Reflection:

Lord, I choose to believe You. There are many things I don't understand, but I'm laying my questions at Your feet and entrusting myself to Your goodness, Your sovereignty. You are who You say You are, and there's more to life than what my eyes can see. Help my unbelief. Keep me. Guard my heart and mind in Christ Jesus.

A BEAUTIFUL LIFE

...Is a Life of Childlikeness

Now faith is the substance of things hoped for,
the evidence of things not seen.
HEBREWS 11:1 NKJV

In the early hours of yesterday morning, the world lost a beautiful person. Ron Core, the music teacher at my kids' school and my daughter's piano teacher, passed away unexpectedly after what he'd called a minor foot surgery. He was in his fifties.

Mr. Core was the best elementary music teacher I've ever seen—phenomenally talented. What's even more important, though, is that I knew he loved my kids. I felt safer, somehow, sending them to school and knowing he was there. The news of his death hit me like the proverbial ton of bricks.

My first impulse was to drive over to the school and get my daughter. I knew she would be deeply affected, and I wasn't sure she needed to be told at school. I first called Mrs. Jones, the principal, to find out how they were handling it.

"We had to tell the kids," she explained in a voice veiled with sorrow. "The story was spreading and we knew we had to manage it, to tell them the truth and help them deal with it."

Along with the counselor and school-based therapist, Mrs. Jones had gone from room to room, assisting the teachers and talking to the kids. My kindergartner, Harper, told me that she cried when she visited their class. "She really loved him," he said, obviously moved by his principal's tears.

Grace, in second grade, said Mrs. Jones talked to her class about Mr. Core's faith and how he was in heaven. "His foot isn't hurting anymore, and he can dance all around," Grace exulted, twirling across the room. "Mrs. Jones said he's probably constructing a choir of angels right now!" She waved her arms like a music director, meaning that he was conducting. I was struck by the delight in her eyes as she pondered these things. Grace was sad that her friend was gone, yes, but her focus was on heaven.

"To understand My kingdom, you have to become like a little child."

That night, after tucking the kids into bed and saying prayers for Mr. Core's family, my husband and I talked about the situation. We both had been melancholy all day, and I was even a little angry. What good could come out of a loss like this? It just didn't make sense. Mr. Core had been a light for Jesus in the school, his community, and all our lives.

Grace's reaction had surprised me somewhat. She's very emotional and deep, and I guess I expected her to cry a lot and be as sad as we were. *Maybe she's just too young to fully understand what's going on*, I decided, and I know there's a level of truth in that. But, later, I felt like the Lord spoke to my heart. He said, *You know, she's the one who really understands better than you. To understand My kingdom, you have to become like a little child.*

It's raining today, and the kids have gone to school, where the music that so blessed their lives has fallen silent. Looking out my window into the gray, it appears that the world is crying. But faith says there's something more going on here—a kingdom beyond what my eyes can see. I'm choosing to receive that kingdom by faith and to walk as a child, even in the rain.

PRAYER AND REFLECTION:

I want to walk in the simplicity of a child today—to trust You with my whole heart and believe the "evidence of things unseen." I know I cannot do this without Your Spirit giving me the power and grace. Like a child, I am dependent on You. I desire to live without worry or fear because You are such a good Father.

A BEAUTIFUL LIFE

...Is a Life of Endurance

*I have fought the good fight, I have finished
the race, I have kept the faith.*
2 TIMOTHY 4:7 NIV

It was mid-August, time for school to start. Being a teacher's kid, a teacher's wife, and a teacher myself, I order my days by the school calendar. On this day, I sat down with my children to discuss our goals for the coming year.

"What are some things you'd like to learn?" I asked Harper, who was then two. "Want to learn to write your name? Count to one hundred?"

"I want to learn to not be scared of granddaddy longlegs," he said simply.

Turning my attention to Grace, who was five—technically school-age—I had loftier academic visions. "What about you?"

"I want to learn to ride my bike by myself, with no training wheels."

My brows began to crease. "What about reading, writing, and piano?"

"I don't care as much about that as I do my bike," she declared. "Will you teach me?"

There was nothing to do but say yes, so we set the calendar aside and geared up for a biking lesson.

We dragged her little bike to the flattest part of the yard. Grace gathered her courage and started pedaling as I steadied her. As soon as I let go, she fell over. Whimpering, she got up, dusted off, and went for it again. For what seemed like hours, we repeated the process.

What stood between Grace and her goal was the sheer willingness to try one more time.

On the second day, she quit falling as soon as I let go, stopping herself instead with her feet. That was good, I told her, but she needed to keep pedaling so she wouldn't stop. She wanted me to run along as she pedaled, acting as a human training wheel. It was backbreaking work, and I finally had to stop.

I explained it was time for the next step, to keep pedaling when I let go. I would give her a good push, and then it would be up to her to keep going. She was terrified, and with good reason—she'd had some tough falls, and her legs were covered with bruises. Pedaling, keeping her balance, and turning—it all seemed like too much.

At one point she was ready to quit, so I gave her a pep talk. "You're almost there! Keep going! It will be worth it!" I jumped up and down like a cheerleader.

She got back on the bike—sweaty, dirt-filled blond hair stringing out from her pink helmet. And that day she did it.

Grace circled on her bike with a smoothness to match her name. We both laughed with the triumph, and Harper cheered like she'd won the Tour de France. It was not yet September, and she had achieved her goal for the year.

Grace's bicycle-riding experience taught me a lesson in falling and getting up. What stood between Grace and her goal was the sheer willingness to try one more time. And just when it was the hardest to try again, she succeeded. How true are Paul's words of encouragement: "Fight the good fight, holding on to faith" (1 Timothy 1:18–19 NIV); "We are more than conquerors through him who loved us" (Romans 8:37 NIV); and "I can do everything through him who gives me strength" (Philippians 4:13 NIV).

Prayer and Reflection:

Lord, I receive Your strength today! Thank You for the encouragement of Your word and for the promise that we are more than conquerors through Jesus. I am ready to fight the good fight, ready to move forward in faith as You cheer me on to the finish line!

A BEAUTIFUL LIFE

...Is a Life of Brokenness

Though He slay me, yet will I trust Him.
JOB 13:15 NKJV

My friend and fellow writer Holley Gerth sent me something she wrote the other day that ministered to me. She's going through a period of brokenness in her life that, among other things, involves the desire to have a baby.

Holley and her husband, Mark, have been happily married for eight years; both have flourishing careers, a lovely home—everything in place, it seems, to start a family. They've done everything they can to make it happen, and many of their friends and family have prayed for years that Holley and Mark could become parents. But so far the Lord has said no.

Here's what Holley writes:

Lord,
Life can be so hard.
We are so fragile...
all of us one breath away from eternity.
We forget until tragedy comes
and we are reminded
how we are all like flowers of the field.

And yet You love us.
You value us.
You gave Your life for us.
But You also allow us
to be broken.
How do we make sense of that?
Where is the beauty in the shattered pieces?
We want You to make
something lovely of our lives
but more often it is more like a mosaic—
beauty out of a million broken pieces—
than the flawless work of art we imagine.
So help us, Lord.
Give us strength in our brokenness.
Let us say with Job,
"Though He slay me,
yet will I trust Him."
Is there a harder prayer to pray?
I do not know of one.
Come to us, take our pieces,
use them for Your purposes
Until we see, as You do,
The beauty in the brokenness.

Although I am a mother of three and my story is not the
same as Holley's, I have my own broken pieces. We all do. Shards
of dreams that have been shattered like glass, broken relationships

we can't fix, jagged edges of our lives that cut us till we bleed. Holley writes that it's those very things—our deepest hurts—that become our ministry. God picks up the pieces and helps us turn them into an altar—a place we can offer sweet, beautiful sacrifices to Him. It's a place where He meets us and blesses us so that, in our brokenness, we can be a blessing to others.

PRAYER AND REFLECTION:

Thank You, Father, for picking up the pieces of my life. In Your strength, I want to build a beautiful altar and offer myself as a living sacrifice to You every day that You give me breath.

A BEAUTIFUL LIFE

...Is a Life of Rest

*"Come to me, all you who are weary and
burdened, and I will give you rest."*
MATTHEW 11:28 NIV

———

*R*obin was a "good girl" who grew up in a good home.
Her family went to church, and she became a Christian at a
fairly young age. Through the years she wanted to stay "pure."
She didn't go through much rebellion as a teenager, unless
you count the time she chose to date a certain boy against her
parents' wishes.

One night when Robin was fifteen, she was babysitting for
some friends. Her boyfriend came to the door, and she let him
in. She liked him and believed he was nice even though her
parents disapproved. She thought they were being unreasonable.

Robin and her boyfriend had a good little visit, drinking a
Coke together and talking while the children played. That's all she
remembers, though. Apparently he drugged her during that time,
because when she awakened later she found she'd been raped.

Before the rape Robin was a virgin. Imagine her surprise
the next month when she found out she was pregnant. In shock
and fear, she told her parents everything, and they took her
directly to a clinic, where a doctor performed an abortion. She
relates that it all happened very fast.

"I watched my life as through a sort of fog," Robin says. "Looking back, I see how passive my role was. I was not a part of the decision to have an abortion; it was just assumed. The decision was made for me by my parents, who thought they were making the best of a bad situation."

When the Lord takes away our pain, He replaces it with His rest.

That bad situation—and Robin's role in it—would define the next several years of her life. After high school, she married and began to build a life that from the outside appeared very happy and successful. But on the inside Robin still struggled. Her heart, always haunted by the past, was never fully at rest.

Robin wanted to believe that God forgave her, but the enemy pelted her with lies. "I thought God might hate me for having an abortion. I believed the rape was His way of punishing me for disobeying my parents and that I was a murderer who wasn't worthy to be forgiven."

Robin filled her life with good things in order to dull the pain. She was active in her community, took care of her home, and tried to be the perfect mother. She searched for answers—as well as absolution—by being involved in her church. Through all of these things, she did find a measure of happiness, but they were like putting a Band-Aid over a wound. The bandage made her feel more comfortable, but the wound never healed. She resolved that she would always have to live with it as part of her punishment. After all, she thought she deserved it.

But God had other plans for Robin. As time passed, He used many circumstances to speak to Robin's heart. There wasn't a mighty rush of wind or a burning bush, but He came to her in simple ways. Through prayer, Bible study, and the love of a few real friends, Robin began to understand the true meaning of forgiveness. 1 John 1:9 says, "If we confess our sins he is faithful and just and will forgive us our sins and purify us from all unrighteousness" (NIV). And in Psalm 103:12, God promises to remove our sins "as far as the east is from the west" (NIV). Slowly, she received those truths into her heart, realizing that if God truly forgave her, it was time to finally forgive herself.

One day Robin prayed a simple prayer: *Lord, I receive Your mercy and grace in my life. I know You forgive me for disobeying my parents so long ago. Even though that choice had horrific consequences, I know it's not true that You punished me when I was raped. I know it grieved You. Your heart for me is love and not hate.*

I receive Your forgiveness for my abortion. Even though to me it is the greatest possible sin, I believe Your forgiveness is greater. Through the blood of Jesus You have blotted it out. Yes, even this sin.

Through You, I choose to forgive the man who raped me, my parents, the doctor, and myself. I place these people, myself, and the burden of my shame at Your feet. I claim the rest that You offer me,

Jesus. From now on, I will rest in Your mercy, and Your love for me. Thank You.

When the Lord takes away our pain, He replaces it with His rest. When He takes away our shame, He gives us joy in return. In Robin's case, when she gave the Lord her past regrets, He restored something in her life beyond what she had ever dreamed possible.

Through special circumstances, Robin heard about a young girl in her community who was struggling in her life. Her father was dead and her mother had abandoned her. The girl was working her way through college and barely had enough money to cover her basic needs. It seemed she was all alone in the world.

One day Robin went to the place where the girl was working in order to meet her. She relates: "As soon as I saw her, I felt this overwhelming love—mother love. I knew, somehow, that the Lord had brought her into my life to allow me to love the child I never had."

Robin and her husband reached out and began to form a relationship with the girl, caring for her needs and becoming like a family to her. The girl's love for them in return brought even deeper healing to Robin's heart. The beautiful bond between them lasts to this day.

Lord, I need Your forgiveness. I need Your rest in the deepest part of my spirit. Wash me in the blood of Jesus. Cleanse me; make me whole. I receive Your mercy and grace, and I rest myself in You.

A BEAUTIFUL LIFE

...Is a Life of Courage

*Then I will go to the king, even though it is against
the law, and if I die, I die.*
ESTHER 4:16 NCV

I like Esther. In a Bible full of books named after men,
she's one of only two women that made the list. That's pretty
remarkable. More significant than that, however, is her courage.

Esther's story begins when King Xerxes gets angry because
his wife, Queen Vashti, won't parade herself in front of his
friends at a party. (She sounds like a pretty brave woman
herself.) He banishes her and then, out of all the maidens in the
kingdom, picks Esther to take her place.

Meanwhile, the king's henchman, Haman, had cooked up
a plan to destroy all of Esther's people, the Jews. It was up to
her to try to save them. But there was one problem: The law
said that anyone who appeared before the king uninvited would
be put to death. Esther knew she faced the reality of death if
she went to the king. In Esther 4:9–11, we see that she tried to
hedge around it, essentially saying, "I'll be killed…. Everybody
knows that the law says the king has to summon me, and he
hasn't done that in thirty days." But her cousin, Mordecai,
convinces her to risk everything. He says, "Perhaps you're here
for such a time as this," and Esther takes those words to heart.

As she plans what to do, Esther seems so brave, so visionary. She tells Mordecai to get all the Jews to fast and pray for her. When they do, God gives her an ingenious strategy that will not only deliver Israel but trap Haman and bring judgment upon him. Esther rises up in courage, counting the cost, and obeys God—even to the point of death. And we all know what happens. God comes through.

Esther's weakness becomes the perfect medium for a display of heaven's splendor— a supernatural courage.

There's no question that Esther is a hero. Something I like about her story, however, is that she is also very human. Very flawed. Esther obviously is not sure what will happen if she goes to see the king. In fact, she's so scared of being killed that she really doesn't want to go at all, even though her people are in grave danger. She wavers, putting Mordecai off at first. She has to be talked into doing the right thing. This is a woman I can relate to. This is someone real.

As humans, don't we do this, too? I don't always respond to a crisis with immediate courage. I wish I did, but sometimes it takes some urging to get me to trust God. And how many times have I asked for prayer or prayed about something myself and then been surprised when God actually came through? I'm ashamed to admit it. Like Esther, I think that sometimes I expect Him to let me down, and it's a surprise when He doesn't. I'm shocked. I don't always know what to do next.

Something important I learn from Esther is that it's not about her, like it's not about me. She could no more control the king's response than I can control the weather. All she could do was be obedient. Courage for her meant putting herself completely in God's hands and trusting Him with the outcome—even if it meant death.

Esther has the impulse—the dream to do something great—but in herself, that's all it is. A dream. Fueled by God's power at work within her, however, Esther presents her request to the king, and her courage saves her people. After that she gets her own book in the Old Testament!

The book of Esther is the story of a powerful queen who lives a beautiful life. But part of her beauty, for me, lies in her limitations. Esther's weakness becomes the perfect medium for a display of heaven's splendor—a supernatural courage. It's not really Esther that does the great thing, after all. It's God. He can do great things in our weaknesses, too.

Prayer and Reflection:

Father, help me to remember that it's not about me—my strengths or my limitations. It's all about You, who You are and what You can do. I put myself at Your disposal today. Use me or choose not to use me according to Your will. I want Your glory and Yours alone.

A BEAUTIFUL LIFE

...Is a Life of Death

Then Jesus said to his disciples, "If anyone wants to follow in my footsteps he must give up all right to himself, take up his cross and follow me. For the man who wants to save his life will lose it; but the man who loses his life for my sake will find it."
MATTHEW 16:24–25 PHILLIPS

My dear friend and mentor, Roy Lessin, has a saying I like (one of many). I find myself using it daily as I'm learning what it means to live a beautiful life with the Lord. The saying is this: *Here's another thing to die to.*

The first time I heard Roy say this, I was sitting in his living room stewing about something that had gone wrong, someone who, I believed, had violated my rights. I can't even remember the particulars now. But I know myself and my tendency to take offense at a perceived slight, whether to myself or someone else, and I know I was mad. Hurt. Disappointed. Something hadn't gone the way I'd planned. Someone hadn't appreciated my contribution or ability. And instead of joining me in my rant about the injustice of it all, Roy simply chuckled. He shook his head. "Well, Gwen, here's another thing to die to."

The words pierced my heart. As I began to consider them, however, I felt a shift in my way of thinking. It was as if I was going down one road at full speed and suddenly Roy's words stopped me in my tracks. I could see where I was headed, and it really wasn't anywhere except frustration. In that moment I decided instead to turn another way—a better way.

How can death be a better way? The idea goes against everything in us; it is the antithesis of the human quest for survival. We think of standing up to our persecutors and fighting for our rights as the American way. We believe that not giving in—not accepting the death of our rights, our dreams, our plans—makes us more free. And there are cases when it does. There are cases when we should stand up and fight.

In Jesus, dying leads us into resurrection life.

But I am learning that, at least in my life, there are many cases when I need to sit down and hush. To lay down my rights. To take up my cross instead and follow Jesus. I may have a right to my opinion, but that doesn't mean it's always right to share it. I may have the right to be angry with my coworker, but that doesn't mean it's always right to tell him off. I may have the right to storm out of the room or the right to treat someone the way they treat me or the right to do any number of things. But that doesn't mean it's *right* to assert my rights.

Jesus said that if I want to find my life, I have to lose it. Sometimes that means dying to a thousand little things a day—

to my own preferences, my own timetable, my own sense of order and justice. It may be as simple as ironing my husband's shirt or as difficult as trusting God when I lose my job. It's amazing how often—and for how many situations—Roy's saying comes in handy!

It's a choice to die to ourselves and what we think we want. And it's not necessarily the easiest road to take. But it's a path to peace, and, in Jesus, dying leads us into resurrection life.

PRAYER AND REFLECTION:

Lord, what would You have me die to today? I choose to die to myself, that You might live Your life in me.

A BEAUTIFUL LIFE
...Is a Life of Resurrection

Very truly, I tell you, unless a grain of wheat falls into the earth and dies, it remains just a single grain; but if it dies, it bears much fruit.
JOHN 12:24 NRSV

The theme of resurrection is the heart of Christianity. We stake everything on the fact that Jesus died for us and rose to live again. As a child, I grasped that truth and received salvation by faith. But it wasn't until later that I began to learn that the theme of Jesus' death and resurrection is played out in our daily lives over and over as we grow in a relationship with God.

The biggest death I've ever suffered professionally was the loss of a job I loved. After changing my major from biology to English, attending law school, and teaching, I believed I'd finally found my niche when I was hired as a writer for a Christian company. I spent a year being trained, investing in relationships, getting perfect evaluations, and reveling in the creative opportunities the position afforded. I thought I would work there forever. Then one day out of the clear blue sky, I was called into a meeting and told that my position had been eliminated; I had two weeks to clean out my desk. My boss seemed truly pained to relay the information, but there was nothing he could do. The company was downsizing.

I was crushed. Looking back now I can see that, among

other things, I was very naive. Clueless as to how the corporate world operated. But I was also about to learn an important spiritual lesson that would serve me well for the rest of my life.

A friend and coworker met me outside after the meeting in which I was terminated. Our building was located near a field that bordered a wood, and there was a little path between the two. A fence separated the path from the wood.

God's way with us many times is through death, but He never intends to leave us there.

We walked down the path in stony silence, both lost in a world of our own thoughts. Mine were a haze of pain and confusion, and I imagine that his were focused on how to help. We sat down together on a bale of hay at the edge of the meadow.

I do not remember anything that was said as we sat there, but I remember looking up through my tears and seeing a deer standing in the meadow. It was looking at me with eyes that burned like coals. As my friend and I stared at the deer, it suddenly started running toward us, gliding, really, across the field. It seemed it might run right over the top of us, but neither my friend nor I felt afraid. Just to the side of the hay bale, it turned and leapt—no, soared—over the fence and disappeared into the forest behind us. My friend and I sat gaping in awe.

After a time, he spoke first. "That deer is a sign to you,

Gwen. I believe you are to view this experience of losing your job as that fence, with you as the deer. Soar past the death you feel today into the resurrection life God has for you, and do not look back."

It took awhile for me to see any fruit from the seed that was planted that day. It had to die and be hidden in a dark place. It had to be watered and sprout into a plant, and now that plant constantly has to be pruned. But the fact that you are reading this book today is proof of the resurrection that has taken place in my life.

God's way with us many times is through death, but He never intends to leave us there. Jesus came to lead us in resurrection life, onward and upward.

PRAYER AND REFLECTION:

Thank You, Father, for the promise of new life that comes with every death. I may not be able to see it now, but I trust You that You are leading me in resurrection life. Guide me, direct me through the dark places, and bring me along in the kingdom of Your light.

A BEAUTIFUL LIFE

...Is a Life of Restoration

I am the resurrection, and the life: he that believeth
in me, though he were dead, yet shall he live.
JOHN 11:25 KJV

When I was in college, I dated a guy I thought I was going to marry, and when our relationship ended, something in me died. It was a dark time. I went through several months of searching—for meaning, purpose, direction—for hope.

One day I went on a drive by myself in the country. I had a fast red sports car, and I opened up the top and just drove. It was the beginning of spring, and though the air still had a cold bite, it was sunny. I drove several miles, praying, listening to music, and feeling the vibration of my car around me. It seemed to hum with life.

I stopped at a church beside the road and parked in the small parking lot. It was a Catholic church with white clapboard siding. The church was very tiny, and the grounds were as neat as a pin. It had a little cemetery beside it that was fenced off, and there were flowers on many of the graves. I'd never been there before. I turned off my car and flipped open my Bible to a random place.

The page I landed on was in Song of Solomon. *Great*, I thought. *The book of love.* Something nudged me to read it anyway, and as I opened my heart, words I don't ever remember reading before began to leap off the page:

My beloved responded and said to me,
"Arise, my darling, my beautiful one,
And come along. For behold, the winter is past,
The rain is over and gone.
The flowers have already appeared in the land;
The time has arrived for pruning the vines,
And the voice of the turtledove has been heard in our land.
The fig tree has ripened its figs,
And the vines in blossom have given forth their fragrance.
Arise, my darling, my beautiful one,
And come along!"
Song of Solomon 2:10–13 NASB

The reality is that the Word of God is eternally true for everyone. But there's also a concept called *ramah*, which means that the Lord can quicken His Word in our hearts in a specific moment today, and that word, in that moment, is for us personally. It's a living thing.

That's exactly what happened to me in my car as I read those words. It was as if Jesus was speaking them directly to me, calling me His darling. *His beautiful one.*

At the time I felt washed out and used up. I certainly didn't feel beautiful, and I wasn't anyone's darling (except maybe my daddy's). But the Lord came and ministered to me that day and filled me with a sense of His love, of how precious we are to Him. I believe He was calling to me to come out of my sadness, out of the death of winter, and into the spring. He was calling me to trust and to place my hope in Him. And it's strange now, but at the time this call had nothing to do with any man. It was a call to arise and walk with Him alone in resurrection life.

The reason that's strange now is that it was that very day when I returned to campus that I connected with my husband-to-be. I had no idea, of course, and neither did he. We both had lots of growing to do, I guess, before the time would be right. But we "bumped" into each other at a meeting, and then the following fall when we saw each other again, he asked me out on a date. We were married a year after that.

When Stone proposed, he dropped to his knees and quoted Song of Solomon 2:10–13. I'll never forget the beauty of that moment, the love on his face. Like often happens in the kingdom of heaven, the restoration that had already taken place in my heart was now manifested before my eyes.

Prayer and Reflection:

Jesus, You came to restore everything the locusts have eaten—to be the fulfillment of every hope of my heart. I can't always see how You are working, but I trust that You are, and I believe You work all things together for good.

A BEAUTIFUL LIFE

...Is a Life of Grace

For of His fullness we have all received, and grace upon grace.
JOHN 1:16 NASB

I teach a class called Introduction to American Literature at a local university. This semester my class examined several slave narratives and discussed them in the context of freedom as an American ideal. At the conclusion of this part of the semester, I invited my students over to my house to watch a movie called *Amazing Grace*. It is the story of William Wilberforce and his fight to abolish the slave trade in Great Britain. The character of Olaudah Equiano, an American slave writer and former slave himself, appears in the movie as a huge influence on Wilberforce's life.

Another major character, portrayed in the movie as the religious figure who shaped Wilberforce's passion for the cause of freedom, is John Newton. He is the former slave trader who, after his conversion to Christianity, denounced slavery and wrote the famous hymn "Amazing Grace." My daughter got her name from that song.

So there we all were, the class and I spread out like old friends around my living room. They range in age from twenty to seventy-two and seemed to be having a good time eating nachos and strawberries with chocolate fondue. My family, who had gone to Granny's for dinner, came in about the time the movie started. Harper and Grace love these occasions and settled in with their bowls of strawberries to watch the movie with us. Grace crawled up in the recliner in one student's lap, and Harper joined me on the couch with another. They were soon enthralled by the movie—we all were.

For this moment,

for this situation,

for my next breath—

Your grace

is sufficient.

As a class we had already talked about the implications of the movie as it related to our readings. Grace and Harper weren't in on any of that. But a few days later, I was riding with my mom and sister-in-law and all our kids, who were packed in the back seats of René's Suburban. I was eavesdropping on my kids, as I often do in these situations, and I heard Harper say to his sister:

"Hey, Grace, you know that movie we watched with Mom's class? I just thought about that song 'Amazing Grace,' and I think I figured out something. You know when he sings 'I once was lost, but now am found, was blind but now I see'?"

Grace says, "Yes."

"Well, he wasn't really blind. But I think what that means is that when he was doing those bad things, he was lost and it was like he was blind and in total darkness. But then when God found him and showed him what he was doing, it was like light came and he could see the truth. Isn't that cool?"

Grace says, "Yes, Harper, that's cool. Now hand me my lip gloss."

I was a little more touched in that moment than Grace was by the magnitude of what Harper had just said. Not only was it so neat to me that he "got it," but as I listened to his wonderful revelation, the truth of what he said opened my eyes again so I could see.

Even though I've never been a slave owner, I know what it's like to walk in darkness. I know—we all do—how it feels to wear chains in different areas of our lives. I love teaching and seeing minds open up and stretch. It's wonderful when I get to help a student gain new freedoms through education. But the message of that song goes much deeper than education. Truth sets us free in our hearts. It *is* cool, Harper! It's amazing!

No wonder I named my kid *Grace*—I need a lot of it. Good thing God never runs out.

Prayer and Reflection:

Lord, I find myself in need of Your grace again. For this moment, for this situation, for my next breath—Your grace is sufficient. Bathe me in it, fill me with it, surround me in grace as I bow my life before Your throne.

A BEAUTIFUL LIFE

...Is a Life of Stillness

*Stand in awe.... Commune with your own
heart upon your bed, and be still.*
PSALM 4:4 KJV

t was one of those moments. A place in time when the
world seems to stop turning on its axis, when everything is
still. You can hear the sound of silence, like all the motion of
creation pauses and catches its breath for just one moment,
anticipating the next spin. Like being poised on the edge of a
star just before it falls, you are privy to all the wonder of the
universe. It's yours to savor, just for that moment. A moment
packed with meaning. A moment ripe with truth. A moment
that will sustain you in other moments, other days.

Blink and you will miss it. Speak and it is gone. Move
and it moves with you, fading on into the past, joining all the
other moments that make up life. Max Lucado calls these times
"eternal moments." And he says you better cherish them when
they come to you. I am happy to say that this time, we did.

We had just heard the news of a family tragedy. My
husband's cousin Eric, age thirty-three, died in his home of
some unknown (until that time) anomaly in one of his lungs.
He had just dressed his four-year-old daughter, Emily, for
preschool, walked into the living room, and fell down dead,

taking his last breath in his wife's arms.

The information sent us into shock. We had just seen him on a recent trip to the town where most of Stone's relatives live. Eric was a jolly "good old boy," who shared with us how proud he was of his daughter and his plans for the future with his job and his wife Tina's beauty shop.

There is splendor in stillness.

Our little family—there were only four of us at that time—sat around our deck talking about the news. We were all so sad. He was the second son Aunt Sue and Uncle Wilford have lost. Such an overwhelming sorrow to be borne, now twice. And poor Grandma and Granddad. How could such a thing happen? It was unbelievable.

Grace was thinking and talking about Emily. Stone was thinking about Eric. And I was thinking about Tina, his sweet wife. Such was the scene on our deck, the four of us, with Harper driving his new car up and down and the river serene and beautiful, flowing on as before, far below us. Occasionally a boat or train went by without noticing us. Leaves rustled. We could feel the gentle breath of the soft, cool wind.

Somehow we quickly and quietly ended up in the hammock. All of us. Stone spread his arms wide, holding me, Harper, and Grace, keeping us from falling out of our somewhat precarious positions. The hammock, though threatening to throw us, also enfolded us like a cocoon and tightly pressed us together. We didn't talk much. Words weren't needed. I believe we all, at some level, felt it. It was one of those moments. We were together, we were alive and healthy and safe, and we let the moment be. We cherished it.

After the moment passed, the heaviness of death and its accompanying grief returned. Stone began to make plans to drive across the state to go to the services. Grace began drawing pictures to send to Emily—"cards." I cooked food and ironed clothes for Stone to take with him. Soon we saw him out the door with kisses, and Grace, Harper, and I headed into town to spend the night with Granny and Pa.

Many lessons can be learned from such situations, I'm sure. Teachers, preachers, musicians, and other thinkers and artists strive to somehow get at the meaning of it all and help us understand. I'm grateful when these insights are shared. For me, however, the greatest lesson this time was found in the hammock. *"Be still. 'Be still, and know that I am God.' I will come and minister to you."*

Some of the things He ministered to my heart were these: Love with all of your heart. Hold on to the ones you love while you have them. You never know when life, like the hammock, may throw you out against something hard and it will be painful. But when it enfolds you like a warm cocoon, don't miss the wonder of it. Beauty—like such moments in the hammock—is ours for the taking, if we have eyes to see it and hearts to grasp it. There is splendor in stillness.

Stone brought back Eric's memorial service program as a

memento. A prayer on the cover expanded the lesson of the hammock further, to things above:

I thank Thee, O Lord, that Thou hast so set eternity within my heart that no earthly thing can ever satisfy me wholly. I thank Thee that every present joy is so mixed with sadness and unrest as to lead my mind upward to the contemplation of a more perfect blessedness. And above all I thank Thee for the sure hope and promise of an endless life which Thou hast given me in the glorious gospel of Jesus Christ my Lord. Amen.

—John Baillie

Prayer and Reflection:

Father, teach me to be still before You. Take me to that place of refuge, that place of calm where You reside in the center of my being. Meet with me there. Speak to me there. Hold me there. No matter how noisy or busy the day becomes, I want my heart to be still and rest in You.

A BEAUTIFUL LIFE

...Is a Life of Confidence

Then Mary said, Behold, I am the handmaiden of the Lord; let it
be done to me according to what you have said.
LUKE 1:38 AMP

ary was a teenager when the angel visited her and
announced that she was to be the mother of God. Her response,
one of total trust, is something that amazes me. She's dazzling in
her simplicity, her purity. On the written page of the gospel of
Luke, her words of submission seem to flow without any effort
or struggle. And yet, I wonder, what was really going on with
Mary, on the inside?

A few verses before this, we find a hint. Luke writes that
when Mary first saw the angel and was greeted by him, "She was
greatly troubled and disturbed and confused." These feelings seem
to dissipate only when the angel says, "Do not be afraid, Mary,
for you have found grace with God" (Luke 1:29–30 AMP).

It seems there was a principle for Mary in the angel's words,
one she would carry with her throughout her life. "Do not
be afraid...for you have found grace." It's God's grace that
would calm her fears in that moment and motivate her to trust
Him...God's grace that would carry her this time, through a
scandalous pregnancy, and also later, through every phase of her
Son's life. His grace became her confidence.

We're not given a lot of details about Jesus' childhood. There's the blessing of the baby by Simeon, when Mary is told that a sword will pierce through her own soul (Luke 2:35 AMP).

And after that, a time when Jesus stayed behind in the temple in Jerusalem after his parents left town. When Mary and Joseph found their son and scolded him for worrying them, he said, "Did you not know that I must be about My Father's business?" (Luke 2:49 NKJV). After that, the Bible says "Mary kept and...guarded all these things in her heart" (Luke 2:51 AMP). Though we don't know everything it entailed, there's a sense that Mary is actively engaged, participating in the will of God—and the destiny of her Son Jesus—all along.

God's grace enabled her to trust Him, even at the cross.

What must it have been like to be there, to see Him beaten and hung on a cross? As a mother, this is where Mary's story touches me the deepest. I'm sure everything in her flesh cried out against the soldiers to save him from such pain. What would it take for a mother to stand there and watch her Son die, offering every grain of strength she had in her to support Him in His mission?

Trust. That's what it would take—confidence in the grace of God.

Mary was not superhuman. She was not pure or strong in herself, nor did she hold herself up as a model for others to worship. Her beauty was not in her glowing résumé, but something much deeper.

She is an example of a real woman who chose to put her confidence in God's character, no matter what it cost. She did not give in to fear because she'd found His grace. And God's grace enabled her to trust Him, even at the cross.

Prayer and Reflection:

Father, I place my confidence in You. You have never failed, and all of Your words are true. There is no one like You. By Your grace, enable me to trust You like Mary did. I am Yours completely. Do with my life whatever You will.

A BEAUTIFUL LIFE

...Is a Life of Quietness

In quietness and in confidence shall be your strength.
ISAIAH 30:15 KJV

There are many things I could say about Janie. She's my mother; I've known her all of my life. I told her once that she is hard for me to write about—not because there's nothing to say, but because there's so much to choose from. Our history together lends itself to thousands of stories of laughter, tears, and everything in between. Today I am thinking of her quietness.

Moma might say *quietness* is a strange word to associate with her. She was an elementary school teacher for thirty-three years. She played ball with the kids at recess, taught them silly songs as well as their lessons, and was no shrinking violet when it came to discipline.

My brother and I can vouch for that at home, as well. Moma brought us up with a good balance of firmness and fun, both of which involved a lot of communication. She wouldn't hesitate to explain things to us. We laughed a lot. But we also understood when things were serious. Moma never believed it was a sin for a woman to raise her voice if the situation was drastic.

The quietness I'm thinking of goes deeper than the tone

of her voice (which most of the time is a nice, even mezzo-soprano). It's a quietness of spirit. I've seen my mother in several situations that try one's soul—and most of the time, no matter how loud and restless the world becomes, she keeps her heart at peace. This has been a great example to me.

I learned how strong— and how beautiful— a quiet spirit can be.

One of the proudest moments I've ever had as her daughter was at a church business meeting. It was one of those disastrous times you hear about, when Christians go crazy and act like they're in a barroom brawl. It's painful to everyone when that happens. In truth, the drama of this night would have been much better suited to any venue other than the sanctuary of God's house.

I watched the arguments unfold in utter stupefaction. The cognitive dissonance between where I was and what was taking place was almost overwhelming. Decent Christian people yelled at each other and waved their arms in fury. I remember thinking, *Has everyone here lost their minds?*

My parents both sat in silence. I know they were as sad and bewildered as I was; many people were. But there seemed to be no helping it. I was crying out for God and needing Him to take control but could hear no voice of peace in the midst of the storm. However, when my mother slowly rose to her feet,

His peace started to break through to my heart.

I don't remember everything she said. What I remember is that she was calm and purposeful—undeterred by the tensions flaring around her. She spoke words of truth in love that brought clarity to a roomful of hazy emotion. From there things got a little more reasonable, and the situation was finally brought to a resolution.

Others may have misunderstood or even disagreed with her for what my mother said that night. But, as her daughter, I learned something that transcended the moment. I learned how strong—and how beautiful—a quiet spirit can be.

Prayer and Reflection:

Jesus, in You I see the spirit of quietness—the gentle strength that comes from knowing Your purpose and trusting Your Father. Give me that spirit today. May I have the wisdom to speak words of truth in love when I should and the self-control to keep silent when it is not Your time. Quiet my heart as I await Your leading.

A BEAUTIFUL LIFE

...Is a Life of Wisdom

*Older women [should] be reverent and devout...as becomes
those engaged in sacred service.... They are to give
good counsel and be teachers of what is right and noble, so
that they will wisely train the young women.*
TITUS 2:3–4 AMP

I met Vena when my husband started working with the
youth at her church. She was the elegant older lady who came to
every service and had wise things to say during open discussions.
I was pregnant with our first child and fresh out of the restaurant
business. We moved into the parsonage of the church.

The parsonage, which was vacant because the pastor had his
own house, was a huge blessing to us. It was right next door to
the church, and so in those years home with my small children,
I got to know several members well who also lived nearby. Vena
was one of those.

Our second child, Harper, had severe acid reflux disease. It
was like colic, but it lasted twenty-four hours a day, seven days a
week, for the first six months of his life. I remember well all the
sleepless nights I walked the floor with him, trying to give him
some relief from the pain. When we did sleep, it was upright
in a recliner—me sitting and holding him in that position—so
he'd be more likely to keep the milk down.

This went on for months. If this story was about me, I could tell you how I came close to the brink of insanity. I never slept, and I felt very inadequate to care for Harper and my two-year-old Grace's needs. Poor Stone, when he wasn't helping with the kids, had to fend for himself. Our lives were completely consumed.

Show me how I might minister to a need today.

One day in the midst of all the madness, I heard a knock on my front door. There were toys all over the floor and dishes in the sink, and dirty laundry spilled out of the doorway of my utility room, which was just off the kitchen. I wasn't expecting anyone and might have panicked at the thought of someone seeing my messy house, except that I was too bone-tired to care. It was Vena.

"Uh, hi, Mrs. Vena," I remember saying, running a hand through my greasy hair. My shirt was stained with trails of spit-up. "Come in if you can get in."

She climbed over baby dolls and puzzle pieces to give me a hug. "How are you doing, hon?"

I told her the truth, which was that I was half nuts.

"Well, I've come to get your laundry."

Amid my halfhearted protests, Vena sacked up load after load of clothes. We dragged them to her car, and she left.

The next day there was another knock on the door, and

Vena was back, with everything cleaned and folded and pressed. Even Stone's T-shirts were on hangers.

I started to cry. "How can I ever repay you, Mrs. Vena?"

Her big brown eyes twinkled. "One day, many years from now, the Lord will give you the chance to help a young mother. When that day comes, remember me."

Prayer and Reflection:

Lord, is there someone You want me to bless in some way? I want to be Your hands and feet and share Your love in the world. Show me how I might minister to a need today.

A BEAUTIFUL LIFE

...Is a Life of Transformation

The Truth will set you free.
JOHN 8:32 AMP

$\mathcal{I}$t was one of those moments. A moment of splendor that comes to us in the commonplace. A moment when eternity injects itself into the present. When something everyday, mundane, is suddenly transformed into something holy and wherever you are becomes a temple of God.

I was standing at my kitchen sink with my arms up to the elbows in sudsy dishes. Grace, my daughter, was sitting on the potty in the powder room right off the kitchen, kicking her legs and singing her little heart out. This scene in itself was a classic, and I laughed to myself at the hilarity of it. Then I registered the words to her song:

> *O victory in Jesus, my Savior, forever!*
> *He sought me and bought me*
> *With His redeeming blood!*
> *He loved me ere I knew Him,*
> *And all my love is through Him....*

Bam. It struck me right through the heart. I love that

song, and her innocent change to the lyrics—from the top of her lungs while sitting on the potty—seemed somehow very profound. The sink became a sanctuary, and light shone forth in my heart as I scrubbed the bottom of a greasy pot.

I am not good at love. Sure, we all have our moments when it comes easy, like when others are lovable. I'll admit that I've been given the most lovable people in the world to practice on. But even with them I find it challenging. I am a selfish being. And often loving another—really loving—requires so much more than what I have to give.

Jesus can and does love others. Through Him it is possible for me.

First Corinthians 13 defines love. It says, "Love is patient, love is kind. It does not envy, it does not boast, it is not proud. It is not rude, it is not self-seeking, it is not easily angered, it keeps no record of wrongs. Love does not delight in evil but rejoices with the truth. It always protects, always trusts, always hopes, always perseveres. Love never fails" (1 Corinthians 13:4–8 NIV).

If I am trying to accomplish this on my own, it may as well say "Love is impossible." But my daughter's modifications to that old hymn reveal the truth that makes it possible. All my love is *through* Him, who is the very essence of love.

This truth sets me free. I cannot love, but He can. I cannot be patient, but He can. I cannot be kind; I cannot help but envy; I cannot swallow my pride or control my anger or forgive or trust again or keep on giving. But *He* can. Jesus can and does love others. Through Him it is possible for me.

PRAYER AND REFLECTION:

Jesus, I can't, but You can! You live in me, and so I have all the love, the power, the kindness, the joy, the patience—everything I need to live a beautiful life. Live in me mightily today!

A BEAUTIFUL LIFE

...Is a Life of Victory

*For whatever is born of God is victorious over the world;
and this is the victory that conquers the world, even our faith.*
1 JOHN 5:4 AMP

’ve witnessed a battle this past year that was as hard-fought and heroic as any epic recorded in history. For all its grandeur, the battle I'm writing about will never be on the news, never celebrated by throngs in a parade. It will never be taught in school or sung about on the radio. There are thousands of battles like it being won today—and thousands lost—that may go unnoticed by the world. It was, and is, a battle of the heart.

My sister-in-law, René, found out she was pregnant with her third child in December. She and my brother were thrilled, as we all were, and wondered if this one might be a boy to go with their two precious daughters.

Around that same time, one of her good friends shared the news that she, too, was expecting. They began to plan and dream about these new lives they would soon bring into the world. Sharing stories of fatigue and unusual cravings, it seemed a special blessing that they were able to experience this journey together.

Then one day René had a strange feeling that something wasn't right. She told herself it was okay, that this pregnancy was just different, but over the course of several days more things happened that fueled her inner sense of danger. At eight weeks, she was ready for her first doctor's appointment. "It will be good to hear the heartbeat," she told me, and I wholeheartedly agreed.

Everyone in our family deeply regrets this now and, looking back, I wonder if we were all in denial, including René. She insisted she could go by herself to the doctor, an hour away, and we truly expected things to be fine. After all, she'd had two very healthy pregnancies. So nobody took off work to go with her. My mother, who is retired, babysat the little girls and waited for René to call.

Greater is He that is in me than he that is in the world!

Alone at her first appointment, René waited expectantly, lying on her back as the doctor did a sonogram. She looked from the screen to his face and back again, watching for a sign.

After what seemed to be an eternity, the doctor spoke. "It looks like the baby stopped growing at five weeks," he said gently. There was no heartbeat.

Opting for the more natural approach, René came home to miscarry rather than having a D&C. The next two weeks were grueling as she waited, knowing that the baby inside her, along with her plans and dreams, was dead.

I believe it was somewhere during this time period that she

reached her most vulnerable point. Call it hormones, call it grief—pain goes by lots of names. But when we are down, our enemy wants to knock us out. I know he waged a full-scale war on her heart.

René and I have a little saying that we got from *Wuthering Heights*. (We like to fancy ourselves like the Brontë sisters, who shared literary aspirations in their own little world out on the moors. That's how we live, sort of, except we're on a farm in the mountains near the Arkansas River.) In *Wuthering Heights*, a character named Cathy Linton declares her love for her adopted brother, Heathcliff, in this very famous line: *"I am Heathcliff!"*

The idea behind that line is that Cathy cannot separate herself from Heathcliff. His joys are her joys, and his sorrows are hers, as well. If he prospers, she prospers; and if he is destroyed, then she cannot survive. A biblical example of this would be David and Jonathan, whose souls were *knit* together. (Our whole family is like this, for better or for worse. Some might call us *thick as thieves!*)

Though my soul is knit with hers, I cannot claim to understand the depth or intensity of René's experience with miscarriage. As much as a fellow soldier can share in a comrade's wounds, I suffered with her. I searched the scriptures for answers. I cried with her. I battled with her and for her in prayer. But the heart of a person is a place no other can truly go. The Bible says we can't even fully know our own hearts. Thank the Lord He has chosen to make this lonely place His home.

In the months to come, I saw Jesus defend René's heart,

drive the enemy back, and begin to heal her. With each emotional conflict, it was up to her to say no to doubt and yes to faith, no to death and yes to life, and no to defeat even as God delivered her the victory, one battle at a time. I never saw her give in to bitterness or envy, even though she admits it was hard on some days.

Her friend has been very kind and supportive through the whole process. About a week ago, René hosted a shower in honor of her and her new baby boy. As I watched my sister-in-law move around the room, filling glasses and making people feel welcome with her warm smile and luminous eyes, I had to fight down a lump that rose in my throat. *This is what victory looks like,* I thought. *Lord, You are so beautiful in René's life.*

PRAYER AND REFLECTION:

Father, I want to walk in victory today. Be hope in me, be victorious in me, be beautiful that others might see You and know You are the way to overcome. Greater is He that is in me than he that is in the world!

A BEAUTIFUL LIFE

...Is a Life of Humility

For the Lord takes pleasure in His people; He will beautify the humble with salvation and adorn the wretched with victory.
PSALM 149:4 AMP

When I was in college, I led a little band of believers from the Honors program in a nursing home ministry. It sounds rather lofty, as I read the words of that last sentence, but the truth is that it wasn't. What it amounted to was a group of kids going into one of the nearby nursing homes about once a week and talking to the people who lived there. We'd also try to coax them out of their rooms and into the social hall, where we gathered around the piano for a few hymns.

My favorite person to visit during these times was an African-American lady named Elizabeth Byrd. I knocked on the door of her room one day at random, and she called for me to come in. She was sitting in her wheelchair, ankles crossed, hands folded in her lap. Her hair was neatly combed back, clothes tidy, and her skin, the color of rich, dark caramel, shone. She wore a dab of wine-colored lipstick, and her teeth gleamed like new piano keys in a wide smile as I sat down beside her.

It was my job to minister to Elizabeth, but as so often happens when we set out to lift another's spirits, Elizabeth ministered to me. She shared memories with me and talked about how the Lord was always with her. How He was her joy and the strength of her life. Her room was like a little haven in that place, and I found myself drawn to it—to the beauty of her spirit—again and again.

Not all the people we encountered were like Elizabeth. There was a lady next door to her who would kick and scream if we invited her to come down to join the music.

"Please, Mrs. Mabel, come sing with us," I remember begging one time, stooped down on one knee beside her chair.

Victory is not in ourselves, whether we're in a pitiful state or a prideful one.

Mabel's white hair went out in all directions like Einstein's, and her face was as wrinkled as a dry river bed. She narrowed her flat, black eyes at me. "I am old and *worn* out!" she hollered, as though I must be hearing impaired. "I am *not* going to sing!"

The group who regularly assembled for music had their favorite hymns. Elizabeth liked "Amazing Grace," and a woman named Lily always asked for "The Old Rugged Cross." Another popular one was "In the Garden." They'd clap their hands and smile, some belting out the words, while others merely hummed along with the piano.

A guy named Perry made a great impression on me during our singing times. He was a tall man with silver hair and a high forehead.

I decided he was a veteran from certain baseball caps he wore.

Perry was in a wheelchair and had to be strapped in it with a wide black belt or he would slide out onto the floor. I don't know what all was wrong with him, but his speech was unclear. He carried pictures with him that were torn out of Sunday school quarterlies. He'd hold them up during the hymns.

Perry's favorite song was "Victory in Jesus." The first time he requested it, I have to admit, it seemed ironic. The question crept into my mind: *What could possibly be victorious about Perry's state?* But I played and sang it anyway. To please Perry, we always sang all of the verses week after week.

It got to where we would always save that song for the last. It became kind of a game with Perry—he would wait with anticipation to see if we would remember, his mouth fixed in a crooked smile. He'd get all excited when I played the introduction, shaking his head to an unheard rhythm. Half the time you couldn't understand what he was saying, but he sang at the top of his voice.

I heard an old, old story, how a Savior came from glory,
How He gave His life on Calvary to save a wretch like me:
I heard about His groaning, of His precious blood's atoning,
Then I repented of my sins and won the victory.
O victory, in Jesus, my Savior, forever,
He sought me, and bought me with His redeeming blood;
He loved me ere I knew Him, and all my love is due Him,
He plunged me to victory, beneath the cleansing flood.

The last time I saw Perry, he was singing that song. Instead of the pictures, he held up both of his arms in a big *V* and formed little *V*s with the fingers of both of his hands. Triple *V* for victory. The next week he was gone.

Now, whenever I play that song at church, I think of Perry. I think of a man in a ruined body whose spirit still remembered how to soar. I think of my question and how he answered it with the words of his favorite song.

Victory is not in ourselves, whether we're in a pitiful state or a prideful one. Victory is in Jesus. I bet Perry sings that song even louder in heaven.

Prayer and Reflection:

Jesus, give me eyes to see beauty as You see it. Help me not to define myself or others by the standards of the world, but to love by Your standards. I need victory in my life today, and I claim the victory that is mine in You.

A BEAUTIFUL LIFE

...Is a Life of Hope

Hope deferred makes the heart sick; but when dreams
come true at last, there is life and joy.
PROVERBS 13:12 TLB

*J*ane grew up in a Christian home and received the Lord at a young age. In her twenties she met Ted, and they were married. Ted was a Christian, too, but neither one of them was very committed. They went to church, but Jane says that apart from church they had a pretty wild lifestyle.

One of Jane's biggest dreams was to become a mother. She always wanted children and so did Ted, and they were devastated when it didn't happen after a few years of marriage. They pursued fertility treatment, spending years and countless dollars on testing, fertility drugs, surgery, and finally in-vitro fertilization. Nothing worked.

After a cross-country move when she was forty-two, Jane searched for a new clinic, new doctors, and a new chance. She found a place, and after a few visits, her name was put on a donor list to receive an egg from a younger woman that would be combined with Ted's sperm and implanted in Jane's womb.

Jane says she drove home from her last visit feeling soul-exhausted. Instead of being hopeful that the donor would be the answer, she was discouraged. "I just felt I had come to the end of the road," she shares.

In her living room that day, Jane sat down on the couch and pored over all their options—all the things she and Ted had tried that had ended in failure and the few choices they had left. It seemed there was no hope for them to have a child, and she felt her dream slipping away.

It was in those moments in her living room that Jane says she heard an inaudible voice. Like sunlight pouring through a window came these words into her heart: *Seek ye first the kingdom of God…and all these things shall be added unto you.*

She knew she'd been doing things her own way, searching everywhere for the solution except the Source.

Jane says she knew she'd been doing things her own way, searching everywhere for the solution except the Source. "God wanted to be my Provider. He wanted me to go to Him for what I needed. I realized that nothing else was going to work."

As she surrendered her heart to the Lord that day, recommitting her life to Him, He began to do a work in her. Listening to His voice and following His leading, Jane felt her connection with the fertility clinic begin to dry up. She removed her name from the donor list. She began to sense the urge to adopt a child and found an organization whose vision for international adoption inspired her.

"It was a long process," Jane sighs. "Lots of red tape to go through and many setbacks." But as she and Ted trusted in the Lord to provide for them, they found the strength to persist for over eight months.

Finally the day came when Jane and Ted would meet their little boy, who was seventeen months old by then and coming from an orphanage in India. A chaperone from the adoption agency would fly with him into the airport near their home.

Jane and Ted gathered with family and a few close friends in the airport lobby at midnight. When the chaperone stepped off the plane holding their baby, Jane says her heart felt like it would burst. Her sister, who was with her, watched Jane's face and said it looked to her like a woman who was giving birth.

Phillip Arfan arrived barefoot, in an ugly T-shirt and ragged black corduroy pants. He peered sheepishly at his new mother and clung to the chaperone, who was familiar. Jane pitched him a little ball she'd brought and held out a stuffed animal. Soon Phillip was snuggled in her arms, warm and safe, and drifting into a peaceful sleep.

In the days to come, as Jane nurtured her son, her body began the change of life. "It was as if the Lord said, *'This is finished.'*" She explains, "I became totally satisfied; my desire to become a mother was completely fulfilled. I never wanted for anything more." A few years later she had a hysterectomy. Jane says her life is a testimony to the truth of Psalm 37:4: *"Delight yourself in the LORD and He will give you the desires of your heart."*

Phillip is twelve now. Saved a few years ago, he followed Jesus in baptism this past Sunday at church. His mother held her own breath as Phillip was immersed in the water. Then, when her son came up smiling, Jane applauded through tears of joy.

Prayer and Reflection:

Father, You are my reason to hope. Thank You so much for Your promises and Your provision. Thank You most of all for Jesus who lives in me—my hope of glory!

A BEAUTIFUL LIFE

...Is a Life of Prayer

*Now there was one, Anna, a prophetess, the daughter of Phanuel,
of the tribe of Asher. She was of a great age, and had lived with
a husband seven years from her virginity; and this woman was a
widow of about eighty-four years, who did not depart from the
temple, but served God with fastings and prayers night and day.
And coming in that instant she gave thanks to the Lord, and spoke
of Him to all those who looked for redemption in Jerusalem.*

LUKE 2:36–38 NKJV

Anna is mentioned only once in the Bible, in the Gospel account of Luke, when Mary and Joseph take baby Jesus to the temple to dedicate Him to the Lord. Simeon is there, a righteous man who was led by the Spirit to the temple, and Luke writes that *in that instant* Anna also shows up and gives thanks to the Lord. She testifies that Jesus is the Messiah (v. 38) to everyone who is looking for redemption. Anna is over one hundred years old.

I can learn a lot from this woman about timing, thankfulness, evangelism, and even aging gracefully. But all of those things branch out from a deeper central stream: The basis for everything Anna is and does is prayer. The Bible says she served God with prayer *night and day* (v. 37).

Imagine this older woman, a widow for eighty-four years,

praying every day without ceasing at the temple. She fasted and told God everything that was on her heart. She probably confessed sin and thanked the Lord for His goodness. I'm sure she interceded for others and listened for God's voice.

This day was, in many ways, like all the others. She was doing her job. Except today the Messiah would appear in the temple in the form of a baby in His mother's arms. And Anna, who had

The basis for everything Anna is and does is prayer.

faithfully yielded her heart in prayer for a lifetime, would be there. She got to see Jesus.

What happens when we pray? It's not so different from Anna's experience. We pour out our thoughts. We confess our sin and offer thanksgiving. We intercede for others; God speaks to our hearts. Most of us could probably benefit from more fasting. But the greatest thing that happens when we yield ourselves to God in prayer is this: Like Anna that day at the temple, the Messiah comes to us. We see Jesus.

Prayer and Reflection:

Come, Lord Jesus; I wait for You. Fill this time of prayer with Your presence. Speak to my heart as I listen. I yield myself over to You.

A BEAUTIFUL LIFE

...Is a Life of Truth

For the word of God is living and active. Sharper than any double-edged sword, it penetrates even to dividing soul and spirit, joints and marrow; it judges the thoughts and attitudes of the heart.
HEBREWS 4:12 NIV

One Sunday morning on the way to church I stopped by my brother's house to deliver something. Leaving my two small children in the van, I went up to the door for just a moment then dashed back down the steps to where my van was running. As I slid into my seat, I shivered. Something cold, thin, and hard was pressed against my neck. Without moving my head, I strained my eyes downward to see that there was a silver blade poking through the space between the headrest and seat. Someone sinister was holding it to my throat. "I've got you now!" he bellowed in a cruel voice.

With a shriek of terror, I turned around to face my attacker. He stared long and hard into my eyes, the blade unflinching, as I begged him to spare my life. With his teeth gnashing, he finally relented. I burst into laughter. My then-three-year-old son, Harper, reluctantly pulled his sword back into his car seat scabbard, and away we went down the hill.

You will rarely catch Harper without his sword. It's the first thing he grabs in the morning (after a sippy cup of milk), and the last thing he relinquishes at night. He carts it everywhere with him, brandished high, as he gallops around on his trusty stick horse. When he's not the villain, chasing his sister with his sword and delighting in her fearful screams, he becomes a handsome prince and bravely declares he will protect her from "robbers… crocodiles…pirates… mooses…" or whatever the enemy of the moment may be. He challenges us all to fencing matches. As he swings his plastic sword, he yells, "Ya! Ya!" and "Get back, you scoundrel!" Or my personal favorite, a quote from Peter Pan: "Take that, you codfish!" When we pretend to fall down wounded, the dark marauder kisses us back to life. Oh, the joy of having a little boy!

May I reach for my real sword, the sword of the Spirit, each morning and meditate on it day and night.

It occurs to me as I watch Harper play with his sword that I have a sword of a different kind that means so much to me. I first came to love it as a little girl growing up at home. It is far more powerful, sharper, and of course more beautiful than any toy. I can take it with me wherever I go, by literally carrying a copy or just by hiding it in my heart. Knowledge of it protects me from enemies of any form—doubt, discouragement, anger, bitterness, jealousy, condemnation, hurt…and I can also use it to speak life into the hearts of those around me.

I am challenged by the fervor of my son for his make-believe sword. I pray that one day he will have the same passion for God's Word. May I reach for my sword, the real sword of the Spirit, each morning and meditate on it day and night. May it never gather dust in my home or heart. May its truth shine so brightly in my life that others will want to read it, learn it, and cherish it and always carry it as their guide through life.

Prayer and Reflection:

Father, thank You for Your truth. I pray You would write it on my heart. Give me a fresh hunger for Your Word and speak to me, teach me through it. Nourish me with Your wonderful words of life.

A BEAUTIFUL LIFE

...Is a Life of Meekness

Then when you realize your worthlessness before the Lord,
He will lift you up, encourage and help you.
JAMES 4:10 TLB

For the full year before it happened, I dreaded my class reunion. A person hopes, if she is going to attend such a gathering, to be skinny, beautiful, happy, and successful at the appointed time. If this is not possible, she can always not go and face everyone. This applies, of course, as long as she is not the president of the class and expected to plan the whole thing.

I could never have ignored that duty. It was one of my campaign slogans back in twelfth grade. I honestly believe it was one of the main reasons I was elected—back then I was thought of as a "very responsible young lady." So, with the generous help of a large number of class members, I set about planning, and the date was set.

When the time came, I was in the midst of moving and up to my ears in boxes. Stone and I were moving out of our restaurant business, as it had closed the same week, and at the time we had one part-time job between us. This sort of state was not conducive to our marital bliss.

I could not find anything, like pictures or other mementoes, nor could I find cute clothes to wear, as I was eight months pregnant and the size of a small elephant. I had one pair of Birkenstocks that fit on my feet, they were so grossly swollen, and those had to go with everything from the picnic to the semi-formal banquet.

In short, I had to will myself to go. Somewhere deep inside, I felt that old sense of responsibility to my class and my friends. These were the people I had preached to about Jesus and the importance of a relationship with Him, how that's what

When I got there, swallowing my pride as I got out of the car, a miracle occurred.

makes your life complete. I had listed a Bible verse as my motto in our senior yearbook: "You have everything when you have Christ…." I had tried to live my life with them as a good friend and a good example, and for as long as I could remember they had supported me by voting me president, along with "Most Courteous," "Friendliest," "Class Favorite," "Most Likely to Succeed…."

Most Likely to Succeed. Cheerleader Cocaptain. The former Miss Ozark High School. Homecoming Maid. For all they knew, I should have graduated from medical school by now and be filling Mother Teresa's place as head missionary to India (this was my senior's prediction at the prom). But, instead, I showed up at an all-time low to my ten-year reunion.

It's hard to explain exactly what happened once I got there.

I don't know what I expected—shock, maybe? Pity? Worse, a smugness that Miss Smarty Pants wasn't quite so smart and together after all? I don't think I consciously expected anything, but knowing the reality of human pride and fear, these thoughts had to be there somewhere in my subconscious. Why else would I not want to go?

When I got there, swallowing my pride as I stepped out of the car, a miracle occurred. I found none of what I feared; all I found was love. Laughter. Acceptance. Even appreciation and understanding. With each hug, each kind word spoken to me or about me to my husband, I began to retrieve pieces of myself that for the past year had been buried. A lot of those people, old friends who knew me pretty well, reminded me of who I was. Not necessarily the most successful, and definitely not the reigning beauty queen, but a daughter of the King who had made a difference in some of their lives.

It was beautiful. It was needed. It was a gift from God to help and encourage me and lift me up.

PRAYER AND REFLECTION:

Lord, thank You for the reminders that I am nothing without You. Thank You, though, that in You I have everything I need. Help me to walk in quiet confidence today—I'm a daughter of the King of kings!

A BEAUTIFUL LIFE

...Is a Life of Devotion

Do everything in love.
1 CORINTHIANS 16:14 NIV

I have seen this with my own two eyes. I witnessed splendor in anguish. I observed two people love each other very much, a mother and a daughter. I was there during the last days of a beautiful life. And I was there, watching with awestruck wonder, as the daughter did everything in love.

It was an honor and a privilege to know Thelma. Though I did not get the opportunity to know her very long, I caught a glimpse of her wonderful spirit and lovely heart. She was a mother, a social worker, a grandmother, a great cook, and a fun person to be around. She enjoyed fishing, shopping, and her family, especially her grandchildren.

I married her grandson and soon discovered that he was crazy about his granny. Whenever we would come and visit his parents in our early years of marriage, we could not leave until we stopped by Granny's so he could give her a hug and a kiss. My husband's sister was equally enchanted with her granny. She wrote letters, called her, and visited with her almost every day.

It is understandable why these two were so in love with her. Apparently, Granny pretty much gave them whatever they wanted all their lives! There were many nights spent at Granny's when they would cuddle up in front of the TV while she made them popcorn and cheese dip. When it was time to go to sleep, Granny would put one arm around each head and pull them as close to her as she could. She never wanted to let them go. They never wanted to let go either.

It was a wonder to watch Janie take care of her mother.

My husband's mother, Janie, had the good fortune to have Thelma for a mother. Janie and Thelma were very close. I really do not have the words to describe their relationship. I could not possibly explain the depth of their love for one another. They had a very special and sacred bond that did not unravel, even in the midst of tragedy.

Thelma had cancer, and not long after she recovered from surgery and chemotherapy, she began to have strokes. It was unimaginable. She had always been such a healthy person. Why was this happening to her? How could this be? There were so many unanswered questions and things we did not understand during the weeks and months and years that followed.

We did not understand why she had to suffer for such a long time. Our family could not grasp the idea of life without her. It was heartbreaking to watch her once-healthy body decay and die all around her. It was a very long and painful good-bye.

Even though this was a difficult time for our family, there

was something gloriously beautiful that shone through the aches and the pain and the tears.

It was a wonder to watch Janie take care of her mother.

If you had been there, you would have seen her honor her mother when she needed it the most. You would have witnessed Janie cook for her, clean for her, and wash her face every day. She wheeled her mother around to go shopping, to the doctor, and to a world-renowned clinic, hoping for a miracle. She wiped her tears, brushed her hair, and read her the paper. Janie did everything she could for her mother. She did it all in love.

For most of her illness, Thelma lived with Janie. Toward the end of Thelma's battle with cancer, she moved to a nearby nursing home. I remember Janie going to see her, bringing her cheerful presents, sitting by her bed, holding her hand, and listening to her. Near the end of the battle, Thelma moved back to her own home for just a little while. That was the place for her to say good-bye. That was the place where she watched Janie grow up. It was where she cooked popcorn and squeezed her grandchildren. It was where we all watched her beautiful life on earth come to an end.

And even then, I watched Janie. I watched her eyes whisper to her mother all of the love she had in her heart for her. She made her as comfortable and safe as she possibly could. She took care of her mother better than anybody I have ever seen. Janie said good-bye to a mother who always told her that she was special, important, and beautiful.

It was a time I will never forget. It was nothing short of

amazing to see the light shine through my mother-in-law. She would be the first to tell you that it was not her light, though. It was the light of Jesus that helped her stay together when everything seemed to be falling apart. It was Jesus holding Janie's hand and comforting her. He was her strength. He was her support.

We never experienced the miracle we were hoping for at the famous clinic. But we did experience a miracle nonetheless. Our family got to see two women love each other to the end. We watched a daughter care for her mother. And we watched her let her go. The miracle of it all is the same miracle we all can have—and that is Jesus.

There is nothing in this world that can separate us from His love. He is always here for us, in happiness and in sadness. We do not have to wait until we get to heaven to experience His love for us. It is right here, right now, for everyone who receives Him. I thank Him for loving us so well and for teaching me, through Janie, how to do everything in love.

PRAYER AND REFLECTION:

Jesus, I thank You that You are always there for me, the guiding force of my life in the wonderful times as well as the hard times. Thank You that nothing can separate me from Your love. Help me, Lord, to give myself to loving others as You gave Yourself to love us all.

A BEAUTIFUL LIFE

...Is a Life of Fullness

*Let your light so shine before men, that they may see your good
works, and glorify your Father which is in heaven.*
MATTHEW 5:16 KJV

When I first met Leota Campbell, she was tall and gaunt,
and in appearance she could have passed for a woman of a
century earlier. She didn't wear makeup. Her gray hair was
combed back from her forehead and gathered in a bun at the
nape. Her garments were plain. As long as she was clean and
neatly dressed, she took no interest in the latest styles. Yet after
I spent several days following her footsteps, I realized that her
lifestyle exemplified inner beauty. She personified the saying
"Beauty is as beauty does."

Leota was a beautiful woman to those who knew her, because
her inner beauty glorified the works that she performed. A native
of Kentucky, Leota came to West Virginia to teach in the public
schools, but she is best known for her many years of service as a
Baptist missionary in the southern counties of the state.

In 1985 I was privileged to compile a biography of Leota,
which was sold by the American Baptist Women of West
Virginia and the proceeds used to establish a trust fund in
Leota's honor. Interest on the original investment continues
to further the education of young people from the area where

Leota served. Even after her death, Leota's beauty lives on in the achievements of those she influenced.

I interviewed several people as I worked on that project and found that those who knew Leota best were good at describing her beauty. Here are some quotations taken from the biography:

Her lifestyle exemplified inner beauty.

Cathy Blankenship, a young woman whom Leota led to the Lord, remembers that, "At Easter, she wears the oldest things she has, for if someone comes to church who doesn't have anything new, she doesn't want them to feel out of place."

A close friend, Emma Eastes, said, "Leota is more like Jesus than anybody I've ever known. She lives in a little trailer, doesn't care to keep up with the Joneses, and doesn't worry about meals. Her main concern is her ministry."

People learn to pray by hearing her pray.

New Christians learn the way a Christian should live by watching Leota. In word and deed, she is an example.

Her ministry is to the poor, the hurt, the downtrodden. So was His. As His, her ministry is caring for people no one else would care for.

Mrs. Ernest Gardner, a pastor's wife, recalled the witness of Leota in the aftermath of a flood in the southern part of West Virginia in 1977 when the Tug Fork River flooded and numerous residents lost their homes. "Leota gave Bibles, storybooks, and literature to the children. At one place, a child picked up some jelly beans off the floor and gave them to us. I didn't eat mine, but Leota popped them in her mouth and ate them, rather than hurt the child's feelings. And the floor never gets too messy for her to get down on her knees. She probably doesn't even notice that the house is dirty or the furnishings out of place—she sees the person."

Leota had many fears, worries, and frustrations, and when I first knew her I considered these to be incongruous with her strong faith and belief in prayer. However, I finally realized that her triumph over those fears made her more of a blessing than if she had no inhibitions or doubts.

She always described herself as "only a clay vessel," but that vessel was a beautiful one because the lump of clay was molded by the Master's hand.

In one of her poems, Leota summed up her life:

Only an earthen lamp
No beauty of design
Come, fill me, Holy Spirit,
Let Christ's glory shine.

Lord, what will my legacy be? Show me how to live so that others see Your beauty when they look at my life. Make me a vessel of Your splendor.

A BEAUTIFUL LIFE

...Is a Life of Service

> *For you have been called to live in freedom, my brothers and sisters.... Use your freedom to serve one another in love.*
> GALATIANS 5:13 NLT

I don't know Camilla all that well; I wish I knew her better. We live in the same community and she has kids around my age, but her kids and I went to different schools so we didn't really know each other. Though our families are acquainted like most families in small towns, our lives might never have intersected had it not been for her husband. He built our house.

I remember the night Stone and I drove over to Guy Richard and Camilla's place. We had set up a meeting to show him our house plans, to see what he thought about building it and how much it would cost. I guess it was an interview, but in my mind he was hired if he wanted the job. I knew I wanted him as builder because he had such a great reputation.

While Stone and Guy Richard discussed numbers at the dining room table, my eyes wandered to the walls. There were pictures of kids and family paraphernalia covering every square inch of space. Camilla, who had already served us ice water, was bringing in groceries through the back door. I remember she had several gallons of milk, and I thought vaguely, *Isn't it just the two of them living here? They must like milk.*

At some point, I left Stone at the table and moved to the bar that faced where Camilla was rummaging around in the kitchen. It was a Saturday night, close to bedtime, and yet she appeared to be assembling a feast. There were baking dishes all over the counters—some full of barbecue chicken, others with beef and several different vegetables.

"Are we in your way?" I asked her, wondering what huge party she must be catering.

"Oh, no!" Her eyes were warm and kind as she wiped her brow with a free hand. "I'm just getting ready for tomorrow."

While I love to worship God at Sunday school, I felt just as near to Him in Camilla's kitchen.

All of Camilla's kids were coming over the next day for lunch—all seven of them—and their families. When I asked her how many people that was, she showed me a framed picture that resembled a small army. I turned to her in surprise, and she just grinned. She seemed as happy as a child on Christmas morning. Furthermore, she told me she does it every Sunday.

"The preacher down at the church came to visit me one time and asked why I never come to Sunday school." Camilla smiled at me. "I told him I can make it to the service, but I've got to cook all morning before that. I believe God wants me to make lunch for my family, and as long as I'm able to do it, I'll be in the kitchen during Sunday school." She chuckled. "I guess when I get too old to cook, I might start going."

This bit of homespun theology might seem outrageous to some people, but it resonated with me. While I love to worship God at Sunday school, I felt just as near to Him in Camilla's kitchen. I'll bet her kids and their kids do, too.

Prayer and Reflection:

Father, show me practical ways that I can love You by serving others today. No job is too big or too small if You are in it; I am willing to serve as You direct me. Help me hear Your voice above all others.

A BEAUTIFUL LIFE

...Is a Life of Worship

And a certain woman named Lydia, a seller of purple,
of the city of Thyatira, which worshipped God, heard us:
whose heart the Lord opened, that she attended unto
the things which were spoken of Paul.
ACTS 16:14 KJV

ydia's story is one that seems particularly relevant for women today who want to live a beautiful life before God. Unlike traditional images we sometimes see of women in the Bible who lived outwardly quiet lives, often in the shadows of their husbands, Lydia is introduced distinctively as a businesswoman who worshipped God.

Now, don't get me wrong. I'm not knocking an outwardly quiet life. After all, that's the sort of life I live. I'm a stay-at-home mom who cooks, cleans, does laundry, irons, and taxis my kids back and forth to school. My husband is the breadwinner of our family. I like to make soup for people who are sick, play the piano for church, and babysit my nieces. Other than teaching a couple of literature classes and writing, I live in total obscurity, way out in the country in a small town in Arkansas. I am certainly not a businesswoman, though I know many godly women who are.

The Bible says to "make it your ambition to lead a quiet life" (1 Thessalonians 4:11 NASB). In our culture, ambition and quietness seem diametrically opposed to one another.

Many women may feel that to be ambitious, they must draw attention to their accomplishments, to "live loud," and, in a sense, make their voices heard. Still others, like some Christian women I've known, seem almost afraid to express their individual gifts if those gifts fall outside the realm of service, hospitality, or mercy. There's a myth that circulates among Christian women in some places that *quietness* means *silence* and a woman's place is always behind the scenes.

Quietness in spirit is the gateway to worship.

Neither view is healthy or accurate. *The Bible Knowledge Commentary* translates *quiet* in the verse above as "a sense of restfulness." It does not mean *silent*, but on the contrary, "undisturbed, settled, not noisy." The writer of the commentary goes on to explain that "Paul was telling the Thessalonians to be less frantic, not less exuberant." While much of the world, including many Christians, seems to judge quietness—or the lack thereof—by what they see women doing, I believe quietness is something more than what's apparent on the outside. I can say from experience that quietness doesn't come naturally just because a woman stays home. And I believe

Lydia's example demonstrates that quietness is not in any way lessened—or hindered—by having a career. The heart of the matter is worship.

I love the word used by Paul in the verse in 1 Thessalonians. *Ambition*. For some, that word may seem out of place in the same sentence as *quiet life*. But the meaning is clear in the story of Lydia. She was a businesswoman whose ambition was to lead a quiet life, evidenced by the fact that she *worshipped God*.

To worship, we have to rest in our spirits. No matter what our calling or gifts, all of us have to be deliberate about it. I do, at home with my kids and the many chores and sometimes chaos that ensues; a businesswoman like Lydia would deliberately have to quiet her heart and meditate on the Lord in order to worship Him. That's what she's doing when Paul finds her on the riverbank praying with other women. And the Bible says her heart was opened by the Lord to receive the truth Paul was teaching.

Whether we as women are called to work outside the home or inside, to be rich or to be poor, married or single, mothers or not—is really not the point, any more than the shape of our noses. Nothing outward makes us ugly or beautiful. What makes us beautiful is when we worship God, wherever we are, whatever we're doing. Quietness in spirit is the gateway to worship—and worship invites Him to open our hearts and fill us with His truth.

Prayer and Reflection:

Here I am to worship You, Lord. Receive my praise and my adoration and let it be a joy to You today. I open my life up to You. Please fill me with Your Spirit and allow me to hear what Your heart wants to say to my heart.

A BEAUTIFUL LIFE

...Is a Life of Giving

God loves a cheerful giver.
2 CORINTHIANS 9:7 NKJV

Before I ever met Cheryl, she gave me something. It was my husband's first year to teach and her son's last year of high school. There was an instant chemistry between Ruston and Stone and me, and we got close to him. He was smart, funny, and mature for his age. We had him in our home several times.

At Christmastime, Ruston came for a visit and brought a little bag. In it was an ornament—pewter angels—and a hand towel embroidered with a dove. "My mom wants to thank you," he said shyly, "for being my friends."

Not long after that Cheryl invited us over. We sat on striped chairs in her living room in front of the fire and bonded with her and her husband, Steve. I don't know if they were testing us—these new people in their son's life—but I guess if they were, we passed. They became some of the best friends we would ever have.

We moved to Gentry shortly after that to be closer to Stone's job. Cheryl had a rental house she offered us, and we planned to move into it until she called us. "I've found something better for you," she said. "You can't move into my little house when there's a nicer one down the street."

I began to recognize this selfless sort of giving as a pattern in my new friend. She came and decorated my house, hauling in pillows she'd made, curtains she'd bought, trinkets she'd found here and there. The delight I felt as I saw my "nest" taking shape around me was second only to the delight I saw in Cheryl—the sheer joy she seemed to get out of giving.

"God's blessed me, and I just feel it's the right way to live."

And it wasn't only me. The more time I spent with her, the more I realized she did things like this for everybody, at least everybody who would let her. Shopping with her became a lesson in gift buying. Christmas, new babies, friends' birthdays, the weather—she was always looking for an opportunity to give.

One time we were out to lunch. We had just been to our favorite store, TJ Maxx, where she'd picked up an assortment of odds and ends. "I know you'll think I'm crazy," Cheryl told me with a surreptitious grin, "but I believe God leads me to things He wants me to give other people. Just look at this great stuff I found!" She dug in her bag, showing me what was for whom and explaining how each thing was the perfect fit for a need she'd seen.

"I don't think you're crazy." I smiled at her. "I believe you have the gift of giving."

Cheryl's gift has been poured out in my life so many times I could never list them all. And while she's blessed my family with countless material things, it's her heart that she's given most of all. In phone calls, e-mails, a road trip to a friend's "just to be together," Cheryl gives away her heart like my baby, Adelaide, gives kisses—free and with abandon.

"How can you give so much?" I've asked her before, knowing there are times her generosity has met with painful rejection and, what's maybe worse, others taking advantage of her. It makes me angry when I see this happen, and I'm amazed sometimes at the way she keeps on giving.

"I can't help it," Cheryl says, like we're talking about resisting chocolate. "God's blessed me, and I just feel it's the right way to live."

PRAYER AND REFLECTION:

Father, I want to be a "giver" and not a "taker." Please show me how. Give me a heart of unselfishness. Bless me that I might be a blessing to others. And thank You so much for all that You give to me.

A BEAUTIFUL LIFE

...Is a Life of Peace

My grace is sufficient for thee.
2 CORINTHIANS 12:9 KJV

As a young mother, Ally experienced the death of someone she loved very much. Although she was a Christian and sought the Lord in the months that followed the death, Ally sank into a depression and even had thoughts of taking her own life. Thankfully, she told her doctor about her struggle and the doctor prescribed an antidepressant that, along with prayer and support from family and friends, helped Ally get back on her feet.

Ally says that her faith was challenged on many levels through this difficult time. She believes one thing the Lord did in her life was to take her to a deeper level of trust in Him—a trust that gives her peace.

"I always wanted to control things," she admits. "I thought that if I did enough, prayed enough, and read my Bible enough, everything would work out. In the case of this loss, it had nothing to do with what I could control. It just happened."

As her world seemed to spin out of control, Ally held tight to the Lord. "It wasn't easy," she says, "and finally I had to face the anger I felt toward Him for what He allowed to happen."

She says that the Lord showed her that His ways are not always our ways, and peace only comes when we trust that His way is best, even when it doesn't make sense. We have to relinquish the illusion of our control and accept His sovereignty, if we want to move forward in kingdom life.

Ally says she still has moments of wanting to protect everyone she loves from bad things. "I was in bed the other night and I started to panic that something bad was going to happen to my children. I felt the Lord speak to my heart, and He didn't say that nothing bad will ever happen. He said that no matter what, He is always with me."

Once it becomes real in our hearts that He is enough, then our peace can never be taken away.

Elisabeth Elliot writes, "God is enough. He may not be all we would ask for, if we are honest, but He is enough." This is a tough lesson to learn, but once it becomes real in our hearts that He is enough, then our peace can never be taken away. No matter what happens.

Prayer and Reflection:

Lord, there are things in my life that I hold too tightly, things I want to control, but I know that is not Your way. It is not the way to peace. I'm choosing to release those things…those people…to You today and to trust You with everything. You are sovereign, You are good, and You are worthy of my trust. I surrender my desire for control to You now, in this moment.

A BEAUTIFUL LIFE

...Is a Life of Love

Jesus said to him, " 'You shall love the LORD your God with all your heart, with all your soul, and with all your mind.' This is the first and great commandment. And the second is like it: 'You shall love your neighbor as yourself.' "
MATTHEW 22:37–39 NKJV

*L*ots and lots of people have a special grandma. In fact, the myriad of names that our society has produced for the word *grandmother* reflects the very special and unique relationship some of us have been privileged to have: We don't just have a "grandmother," we have a nanny, a memaw, a mamaw, or a granny. And I was in no way an exception to this unwritten law: I had a GaGa. When my toddler lips could not fully form the word "Grandma," what eeked out instead was this two-syllable infantile word that stuck like molasses taffy: GaGa. My grandmother fell hopelessly in love with her new name, and that was that!

GaGa had only one son and two granddaughters. Sadly, her husband had abandoned her w–a–a–y before I was even born. So it doesn't require great leaps to imagine how readily and easily her granddaughters became central to her life. She spoiled us in every way she possibly could with her meager income, and I never took her love and devotion for granted. She was equally as special and central to my world, as well.

GaGa didn't have much wealth or worldly treats to share with us. She hadn't had an inheritance from her poor parents to build upon. She didn't have a dozen pair of shoes, a fancy coat, or a nice car. She never had central heat and air or a dishwasher. She never took a vacation to the beach, to the mountains, or even to closer destinations in our humble state. Yet I never once thought of her as poor. She had more friends than anyone I have ever heard of! It was rare to be at her home without one of them "dropping by." Her phone produced a steady ring of friendly callers, too, and every year her Christmas tree was practically strangled by the number of gifts from my sweet grandma's many friends.

It was never about her selfish interests or ambitions, it was about everybody else's.

GaGa had a way of making everyone in her life feel special. Whenever you'd call her, she would generally say, "I was just thinkin' about you!"—and she undoubtedly was. You see, GaGa wasn't all about herself; she was about *the people* in her life. It was never about *her* selfish interests or ambitions, it was about everybody else's. It is this quality that endeared her not just to me and my family but to our entire community.

It was with great anticipation that I prepared to interview

my grandmother on a borrowed video camera. She was in her seventies and, as far as I could tell, a monument in our town and in my life. I was thrilled at the prospect of capturing her witty charm and abundant love on film. At the end of the interview, I asked one last pointed question: "GaGa, do you have any advice for future generations?"

I fully anticipated her to say, "Love God with all your body, mind, and strength," for she surely did, and I was sure she would want her grandchildren and great-grandchildren to do the same. If she didn't say that, I was certain her answer would be: "Be the best person you can be, all the time and every time," for she had certainly led a life of endurance and perseverance. You see, I thought I knew what she would say to capture her life's essence. While what she did say was not in opposition to these ideas, it touched me deeply and continues to affect me these many, many years later.

"Just love everybody. Help everybody all you can."

PRAYER AND REFLECTION:

Jesus, You told us to love You and to love our neighbors as ourselves. You said it's that simple; that's what sums up the whole law. But it is so easy for me to get caught up in other things. Help me stay focused today on what You think is important—and keep me mindful that to be Your disciple means that I love others. Flow through me like a river; love others through me with Your unconditional love.

A BEAUTIFUL LIFE

...Is a Life of Faithfulness

Because of the LORD's great love we are not consumed,
for his compassions never fail. They are new
every morning; great is your faithfulness.
LAMENTATIONS 3:22–23 NIV

One morning during the worst season of my marriage, I woke up to find this verse in bold letters hanging on our refrigerator. My husband had put it there as a reminder to me and, I'm sure, to himself, that God had not forgotten us.

We'd sung all the verses to "Great Is Thy Faithfulness" at our fairy-tale wedding, where we were described as a "power couple" by various friends from college. Successful socially as well as in academics (and he in sports), we started our marriage on the crest of a wave that, it seemed, we'd be able to ride forever. Six years later, however, we were without jobs, broke, and searching for God's direction.

We'd taken a leap of faith, thinking we were embarking on a great spiritual adventure. Only, as sometimes happens in such adventures, we fell flat on our faces. After several months with seemingly no answers in sight, we ended up in my hometown running a café/bed and breakfast. We lived in one bedroom on the premises. Stone went from head coach to head waiter. And I used all of my education and expertise to chop salad ingredients in a sweltering kitchen. Three months into this experience, I found out I was pregnant. These were not exactly the ideal circumstances we'd envisioned for starting a family.

I learned many, many lessons in that season—enough to fill another book. But the most important one is that God is faithful. The Bible says that even "if we are faithless, he remains faithful" (2 Timothy 2:13 NRSV). Even when we miscalculate and falter in our faith, even when we mess up. In time He provided the way of escape—a new job and a ministry for Stone, writing assignments for me, and a whole house where we could live and raise our baby.

Looking back now I can see how He was at work—even in that dark time.

At times the Lord seems silent, but He is always there, blessing and keeping us in His eternal love. Looking back now I can see how He was at work—even in that dark time—to bring things together for our good. Deuteronomy 33:27 reads, "The eternal God is thy refuge, and underneath are the everlasting arms." Whether you're soaring like an eagle or falling toward rock bottom, Jesus is there to catch you. His faithfulness will never fail.

Prayer and Reflection:

Thank You, Lord, for Your faithfulness to me. You have never failed me, and You never will. Help me be faithful to You.

A BEAUTIFUL LIFE

...Is a Life of Simplicity

It is the Spirit that gives life. The flesh doesn't give life.
The words I told you are Spirit, and they give life.
1 PETER 3:4 NCV

A beautiful life doesn't require lots of money or fancy clothes. It's not a life of ease and extravagance, nor is it a life of striving for success. A beautiful life can be lived by any ordinary person in any ordinary place.

I know this to be true because one of the most beautiful lives I've ever encountered was shared with me in my hometown of about three thousand people, in a normal house on a normal street. I used to go there once a week for piano lessons.

When I met Gail, I was in the first grade, and I was shorter than her dog Anheuser. He was a St. Bernard who would greet me at the back door, sliming me on the face with his enormous pink tongue as I ran past, trying to dodge him on my way to the piano.

Gail would meet me in the living room. For thirty minutes or so she'd sit beside me in a beige chair and listen as I tried to play whatever songs she'd assigned me the previous week. Sometimes she'd take over the piano, demonstrating a difficult section of the music or sharing something new with me that she was practicing herself. She was our church pianist, and she made magic out of ordinary hymns. Her hands shook from a neurological condition, but the shaking never seemed to affect her amazing skill and tone.

I can still see her sitting in that chair beside the piano, watching me through her dark-framed glasses. What she must have thought sometimes of my lack of practice or the strange phases I went through as a teenager… Her lessons were a balance between tough and tender—a wise teacher's effort to push a student, but not too hard.

Gail's journey is one of cultivating deep inner beauty in herself and those around her.

As the years passed, so eventually did Anheuser, and I grew up. Spending thirty minutes with Gail each week playing the piano was one of the few things in my routine that never changed. By opening her life to me, she taught me many lessons that go beyond the piano. The most important was what it means to live by the Spirit.

Gail's life hasn't been easy. In fact, if you looked at her condition from its outward appearance, you might never see the beauty inside. Her only son was struck and killed by lightning. Her husband, whom she adored, fought with demons that sought to destroy them both. Even now she lies in a bed at home, where for years she's been dealing with cancer and unable to stand or even sit for more than a few minutes at a time.

Through everything, Gail remains faithful. She chooses to draw life from the Spirit instead of dwelling on what's wrong with the flesh. I visited her not long ago and had to ask, "How do you handle having to lie in bed all day long?"

"Well, I don't like it," she grinned, spunky as ever. "But I know the Lord is in control. I trust Him to take care of me." She quickly changed the subject to intercessory prayer and how I might join her in praying for someone she knew who was in need.

This response, so typical of her, is one that challenges and inspires me, just as her life always has. Gail's journey is one of cultivating deep inner beauty in herself and those around her. Just as she did with me all those years, thirty minutes at a time.

Prayer and Reflection:

Father, purify my heart today. Take my eyes off my circumstances, the good, the bad, and let me see You. Help me to simplify my life so that nothing gets in the way of my relationship with You. I want Your beauty in my inner self—I want You to be at home in my heart.

A BEAUTIFUL LIFE

...Is a Life of Light

Godliness with contentment is great gain.
1 TIMOTHY 6:6 KJV

*M*y name is Charlene Lessin. I grew up on a farm in a small Lutheran community in Minnesota, where I had a wonderful childhood. My parents were committed Christians who planted Bible truths into my life, and we were very involved in our local church. I was a "good girl" who knew a lot about the Lord, but I'd never come to know Him personally.

Upon graduation from high school, I went to college at Bethany Fellowship. When classes began my first year, I would go to one class and hear, "Jesus loves you. He not only loves the world, but He loves you." I knew He had died for the world, but I began to understand more and more His love for me personally! In another class, the teacher would say, "Being good is not enough; you need Jesus." Still other classes taught the same message: "Even though you've gone to church and tried to do right, it's through Jesus that your sins are forgiven and you find salvation."

This went on for three months. One day I heard someone read the Bible verse that says all of our righteousness is as filthy rags (Isaiah 64:6). I realized that all of my efforts to *be* good and to *do* good could not save me and could not impress God for my salvation. Shortly after hearing that verse, during one of our classes, I felt the guilt of sin heavy within me. The Holy Spirit was showing me my need. I trembled at my desk, trying to ignore what the Lord was revealing to me.

I had experienced a tug at my heart similar to this while I was in high school. My dad took me to the Pelican Rapids high school auditorium for a Billy Graham film geared for young people that was showing one night. As I heard

There was a need for God's love in my heart and life, and only He could fill that with Himself.

parts of the story and singing, I sensed deep within that what I needed was what the film was sharing about the gospel of Jesus. But I did not respond at that time. Now I knew clearly, without a doubt, what I needed to do to get rid of the nagging fears and guilt of sin. All my trying to be good was not enough. I was a sinner, and I needed a Savior. I needed Jesus.

By this time I had become part of a girls' trio, and we sang at a Sunday night service. After the sermon that night, the preacher asked if anyone had a need and would like prayer. I knew what I had to do. I went to the front where our dean of women, Mrs. Hegre, joined me and led me to the choir room for privacy. I wept, knowing I was a sinner, and I repented of my sin and cried to the Lord to save me and to come into my heart and life.

In that moment it was like a ton of bricks fell off my shoulders, and I knew that Jesus had accepted me and come into my life—with His life—by the Holy Spirit! All the songs that I had sung about Jesus' love for me throughout my childhood became very real in that moment. I had a lot to learn in my new walk, but I had such peace and joy, knowing for sure that I was right with God.

How could it happen that this girl who was raised in such a good home, with wonderful parents and raised in church, did not understand these things earlier? I don't know, except I do know that whoever we are, black is black, and I was in the blackness. If you live in a mud hut or in a castle, when the lights are all out, it is black.

I remember being a young teenager lying on my bed and trying to pray to God, but my words bounced back to me like the ceiling was made of thick iron. I remember going to the pasture to fetch the cows for milking one day and looking up into the sky, wondering if God knew I existed. I felt sure He didn't!

I thought that maybe I needed to become a nurse or a doctor; then He might recognize me. Maybe I was just to live life with no meaning at all. Though outwardly my life was good, inwardly I felt very insecure and lonely and sad. I couldn't see any hope for the things I felt within, and I didn't see any way out of this darkness, even though I was surrounded by love and goodness from my parents and others. I thought I had to become something that I knew I probably never would accomplish, like working on the mission field.

Everybody else had a purpose, but I didn't. God knew everyone else, but maybe He didn't know me. I later came to learn that these ideas were all lies.

To answer my earlier question in all honesty, I would have to say it was no one's fault but mine that I didn't understand. I was inwardly a proud person, and I couldn't clearly hear the Lord's voice for many years until I came face-to-face with some heart issues there in my classes. It was not that I had robbed a bank to realize this, but the Lord showed me that my own way, my pride and my selfishness, kept me from knowing Him. It was then, as a result of my parents' and grandparents' prayers, I'm sure, that the Holy Spirit opened my eyes to see my need. I was just turning eighteen years of age.

I thank the Lord over and over that He revealed to my blind eyes my need and He was the answer! I have learned through the years that even though people loved me, there was a need for God's love in my heart and life, and only He could fill that with Himself. Religion can't fill it; traditions can't fill it; good works can't fill it. Only Jesus can fill it.

I came to know in reality what the song we sang in Sunday school every Sunday meant. *Come into my heart, Come into my heart, Come into my heart, Lord Jesus. Come in today, Come in to stay, Come into my heart, Lord Jesus.*

Wow, what a joy to be able to walk around each day with that load of bricks gone! To walk each day in the Light!

Now, over forty years later, if I were to sum up in a few words what the Lord has done for me, it would be this: I am continually amazed that I could come to know Him. His provision on the cross was for me as well as for the world.

At one time in my life, I was so proud and sure of what I could do and accomplish, but He took me to a place where I learned that I couldn't but He can. That is the best place to be—where we recognize that *He can*. Knowing Him and His presence makes my heart cry out, "I'm so grateful! Thank You, Jesus!"

PRAYER AND REFLECTION:

Thank You, Jesus, that You came for me. Thank You that Your light shines in my life and Your presence is always near me. I'm so grateful, and I want the world to know what great things You have done.

A BEAUTIFUL LIFE

...Is a Life of Faith

I am calling up memories of your sincere and unqualified faith
(the leaning of your entire personality on God in Christ in
absolute trust and confidence in His power, wisdom, and
goodness), [a faith] that first lived permanently in [the heart of]
your grandmother Lois and your mother Eunice and now, I am
[fully] persuaded, [dwells] in you also.

2 TIMOTHY 1:5 AMP

It is interesting to me how these two women made their mark on the world. We don't know anything about how they looked, what their natural talents were, or what they did for a living. This is the only verse in the Bible that even records their names. But in it, we are given a snapshot of beautiful lives—the lives they lived and the life they passed on to Timothy.

Notice that it is not Timothy's father Paul mentions in his letter. It's not Timothy's teacher, playmate, or his best friend. It is his mother and grandmother who are noted for their faithfulness, to Timothy and to God.

What does the snapshot look like? There's an old woman, Lois, and Eunice, who is probably middle-aged. A young man stands between them with a sack slung over his shoulder, as though ready to embark on a journey. He is smiling. He has been chosen to assist the most powerful missionary in the world.

The verse above also gives us a clue as to why Timothy was chosen. Paul says that a "sincere and unqualified faith"—"the leaning of [his] entire personality" on Jesus, with "absolute trust in [His] power, wisdom, and goodness"—dwells in Timothy. Wow. And it "first lived permanently" in the hearts of Lois and Eunice.

How might that faith have been lived out in these women's daily lives? The Bible doesn't say, but I can imagine. Perhaps there was a time when Timothy fell and scraped his knee and Eunice held him in her arms, wiping the scrape clean with cool water and telling him the story of how Jesus washed His disciples' feet.

Make me a servant, a faithful reflection of Your beauty, in the lives of others.

Maybe one day Eunice made a meal for someone who was sick and Timothy got to help even though he made a mess in the kitchen. Maybe she took him with her to deliver the meal.

I'm sure there were times when Timothy tried their patience by bringing unwanted animals into the house or not picking up his things. Maybe Lois and Eunice were always loving. I doubt it, though. No human always is. Maybe they got angry and yelled at him sometimes but had the wisdom to apologize later. And maybe he learned humility from that.

I imagine that Lois and Eunice gave Timothy lots of hugs.

I bet they taught him how to pray. I bet they sang to him and disciplined him and played with him. And I bet he learned a lot of things from them when they thought he wasn't looking.

We don't all have kids and grandkids, but all of us have a life. We have people around us who fall and hurt themselves and people who are sick. We have people who try our patience, people who need a hug, and people who watch us when we think they're not looking. We have people who need to hear us singing and people we need to stand up to. People we need to laugh with and people we can point to God when times are hard.

I believe that's the legacy of Lois and Eunice and the way faith transfers from one life to another. One beautiful moment at a time.

PRAYER AND REFLECTION:

Father, as I go through my daily life, I want to leave a legacy of faith. Please lead me in the way You want me to go. Direct my every step so I don't miss the opportunities You give me. Make me a servant, a faithful reflection of Your beauty, in the lives of others.

A BEAUTIFUL LIFE

...Is a Life of Thankfulness

Give thanks unto the LORD; for he is good.
PSALM 106:1 KJV

As the expression goes, I turned thirty-six this year.
Turned, like a leaf turns colors, like one turns the pages of a
book or turns down a new road. The road out of my thirties
is one I'd like to take slowly, but as someone rather rudely
reminded me, "Thirty-six rounds off to forty." I can already see
forty around the bend, and even fifty and sixty don't appear too
far away.

This "turning" has been a time of reflection for me. Route
thirty-six has many good places to stop and ponder over the
years of my life and to consider what they have meant, what
my life has been. This pondering has been a most rewarding
experience.

Of course, when I look in the mirror there is the realization
that I don't look just the same as I did in my twenties, and
when I play with my children at the park I see that even my
relatively young body is not as young as it once was. (I got stuck
on the monkey bars and fell flat when I tried to jump out of a
swing.) These things are undeniable. But are they real losses at
age thirty-six? No. My seventy-two-year-old aunt would laugh

me to shame at any other answer.

Naturally, taking another honest look—a little deeper—reveals a few regrets. Have I made all of the best choices? Spent all of my time wisely and with the most enriching or worthy people? No. Have I gone to all the right places? Said all the right things? Have I always given my utmost to and for the God I love? No, no, no. Sadly but truly, no. Again, these facts are unfortunate and as undeniable as the crow's feet I see in the mirror.

You have been so good to me, Father!

However, as I walk down this new road called thirty-six, the view I see behind me is overwhelmingly beautiful. Marred though the landscape may be with what are thankfully few regrets, it is a breathtaking sight. Pausing, pondering, its loveliness envelops me, fills me, warms me, rises up in me, and catches like a sob in my throat.

I see all the people who have shared my journey…my parents, my brother, my grandparents, and other family. Their faces beam at me as I look back. A fresh-faced couple with newborn me as their prize, a baby brother to cuddle and love, a man in a straw hat with pride glowing in his big brown eyes, a woman who made the best homemade rolls ever.

I see others who loved me and helped me find the way… school teachers, Sunday school teachers, music teachers, friends. College professors, my husband and babies, my in-laws, colleagues at work. These are the ones who shine like stars on the horizon of my life. They are the gleaming, resounding answers to the questions of what my journey has been. They rise above any regrets I have and soar like eagles on the wings of joy.

I am grateful for the life I've lived so far. It has not been perfect—but it has been a blessed, wonderful, extraordinary life. The experiences afforded, lessons learned, goals accomplished, and most of all the relationship with God and others, can only be defined as abundant. The theme of my thirty-sixth year, and I pray to the end of my road here on earth, is thankfulness.

Prayer and Reflection:

You have been so good to me, Father! You are faithful and wise and so loving. Thank You for all the things You have done and where You've brought me. And most of all thank You for You.

A BEAUTIFUL LIFE

...Is a Life of Unity

Behold, how good and how pleasant it is for brethren to dwell together in unity!
PSALM 133:1 KJV

———————

hinking about the beauty of unity takes me back to an experience I had a few years ago with believers from a different denomination than my own. I was asked by a friend to help out with a Christmas musical at her church. I had no experience directing a choir, but I do read music, which was what she said they needed. So I said I'd give it a try.

I showed up the next week at the Bread of Life Fellowship for practice. It was quite intimidating. I stood in front of about twenty people, mostly adults who were older than me, as they sang the songs. I read along in the book, trying hard to keep up.

I had a nagging fear they would see that I didn't really know what I was doing. I remembered from my drum major days in junior high band how to mark time, so I started waving my arms to the beat. I sang along. By about halfway through the program, I was completely swept away by the music. The kind and eager faces of the singers looking out at me won my heart and gave me courage. I began to have *fun*!

Each week I looked forward to the practices. When I entered the church I was greeted with smiles and encouragement. I learned the names of the singers and felt a sweet camaraderie with each one. They were so patient with me and open to my instructions. The sound man was always there to stop and do it over, stop and do it over—every time I yelled "Cut!" We had lots of laughs and did a lot of hard work. Every night after practice I left mentally and physically tired but also strangely energized and fulfilled.

What a beautiful thing it was for me to stand in unity with other believers.

There were two performances. When the time for the first one came, we met early to pray and warm up our voices. It was pouring down rain and cold outside, but in that little church on those dark nights there was a warm fire glowing in us. When the music began, our spirits started to soar and I forgot everything else around me except for the lovely faces of those singers and the hearts behind them. They sang like angels and I, their lowly director, being ushered into the meaning of Christmas, lifted my hands and truly worshiped Christ, the newborn King.

I am hesitant to make the statement, as some will about different things, "That's what Christmas is all about." How can we, as finite beings, ever comprehend what it is all about? But I have the distinct impression that one thing Christmas is about is unity. What a beautiful thing it was for me to stand in unity with other believers—not of my same denomination, but of the same Lord. A choir of different voices blended together in perfect harmony. How sweet the sound! I believe with all my heart that it was music to His ears.

PRAYER AND REFLECTION:

Father, help me to be a peacemaker among Your people. I pray that I would never build walls that keep people out, but that in Your wisdom I would build bridges. Help me not to judge. Help me be open to what I can learn from others and their journeys with You. Guide me in Your truth and teach me how to walk in unity with other believers.

A BEAUTIFUL LIFE

...Is a Life of Sacrifice

But Hannah did not go, for she said to her husband, I will not go until the child is weaned, and then I will bring him, that he may appear before the Lord and remain there as long as he lives.

1 SAMUEL 1:22 AMP

My husband speaks at our church sometimes, and he occasionally likes to dress up like a Bible character. One Sunday he pretended to be Samuel and told the story of how his mother, Hannah, prayed for a child and when God answered her prayer, she dedicated her son to Him at the temple.

That afternoon we were talking about the service around the dinner table. My little son, Harper, looked me earnestly in the eyes. "Moma, would you ever take me to the temple and leave me there, like Hannah did?"

I had to answer him in honesty. "I don't know." While he waited, I thought about it further. "No, as a matter of fact, I don't think I ever could do that."

We explained to the kids that Hannah believed that was what God wanted her to do. Samuel was safe at the temple, and he was learning how to serve God. He became a great spiritual leader for Israel. That seemed to satisfy them.

In my mind I kept going back to Harper's question, though.

Sometimes we read stories like Hannah's or Abraham's, or we've heard them all of our lives, and they feel sort of distant to us. Something that happened a long time ago to people who were different than us. What struck me about Harper's question was the freshness of perspective. He immediately related it to him and me, and that made it so much more real. No longer was it just that Bible story about Hannah and Samuel. It was, *What if God asked me to make a sacrifice like that with my own son?* I realized what a huge sacrifice it must have been for Hannah. She accepted God's will and obeyed Him even when it cost her everything. My gut reaction was that I could never be like her. I could never do that.

Sacrifices don't always have to be huge.

I have to admit that I have problems with a story like Hannah's. It's almost as difficult for me to grasp as the story of Abraham and Isaac. I believe God is sovereign and completely loving. But in the natural, neither one of these stories makes sense. Surely other honest people read them and think, *Huh? God asked these people to do what?* Just like today when someone is suffering with a disease or we lose someone we love—it's hard to accept.

Hannah—and Abraham, for that matter—waited so long for a child. She had prayed and longed for Samuel. She loved him like I love my children. It would never be possible for me to willingly give up one of them, to only see them once a year. No matter how many other children I had, I would not want to part with a single one. Yet that's what Hannah did. She turned Samuel over to Eli the priest to raise.

Thank the Lord, we're not typically asked to sacrifice so much. My husband and I dedicated our children to the Lord soon after they were born. We want them to live God's purpose for their lives, and we're teaching them to listen to His voice. Along with extended family and church friends, their spiritual training is up to us, and that's the way I like it. It's not exactly what you'd call a sacrifice. It's our delight.

But sacrifices don't always have to be huge. My sacrifices lately come more in the form of preferences—something I want to do, somewhere I want to go, some material thing I want to own. Or maybe it's just having my selfish way about things. The closest thing I've come to Hannah's story is probably that manuscript I'd love to see turned into a best seller or even a movie. What if God comes along and says to lay it down? To give it up? Could I do it?

Not in my own strength. In my own strength I'm not good at sacrificing anything. But 1 Samuel 2 lets us in on Hannah's beauty secret:

Hannah prayed and said,
"My heart exults in the LORD;
    my strength is exalted in my God.
…I rejoice in my victory.
"There is no Holy One like the LORD,

no one besides You;
   there is no Rock like our God....
The bows of the mighty are broken,
   but the feeble gird on strength....
He raises up the poor from the dust;
   he lifts the needy from the ash heap,
to make them sit with princes
   and inherit a seat of honour.
For the pillars of the earth are the LORD's,
   and on them He has set the world.
"He will guard the feet of His faithful ones,
   but the wicked shall be cut off in darkness;
   for not by might does one prevail.
The LORD will...exalt the power of his anointed."
1 Samuel 2:1–2, 4, 8–10 NRSV

PRAYER AND REFLECTION:

Father, it's in Your strength that I can sacrifice my desires, my wants, my ways for the good of Your kingdom. Make me strong in You so that I can be willing to do whatever You ask—no matter what the cost.

A BEAUTIFUL LIFE

...Is a Life of Joy

The King's daughter is all glorious within.
PSALM 45:13 NASB

A few years ago, the book *Captivating* by John and Stasi Eldredge struck a chord among thousands of women. The thesis of that book is that women need to know they are "captivating" to the Lord—that He finds us not only acceptable, but wonderful, beautiful, and appealing. The authors note that this can be difficult to believe when one has not been nurtured as a little girl by her father. In fact, many women have wounds from their earthly fathers that only God can heal.

I'm blessed to have a father who has always made me feel loved. His nickname for me is "Pretty," and he's shown me all my life that he sees me that way—on my best and worst days. Another man in my life who taught me my value was a Sunday school teacher I had as a child who was also a friend of our family. He'd always ask the girls in our class, "How'd you get so beautiful?" And we'd have to say, "God made us that way." No other answer was acceptable.

One time I questioned my teacher about saying that God made me beautiful. "Isn't that like bragging?"

He looked at me and smiled. "You're not bragging on

yourself. You're bragging on God."

Another thing both he and my daddy always told me as a child is that I was a daughter of the King. There are moments when I can still hear both of their voices in my head, declaring that truth when I need to hear it most—in those moments when happiness flees and I don't feel anything like beautiful or royalty.

Our beauty is not based on something we can do or even the looks or brains we've been given.

I'm trying to pass this truth along to my own Sunday school class. I meet with the teenage girls at my church once a week, and this past month we made two life-sized paper dolls. One is named "Iman Object," and she is decorated in a collage of pictures we cut out of magazines. She's glitzy and glamorous, sexy and sophisticated. She wears lots of makeup, skimpy clothes, and has perfect hair and teeth. On the outside she represents the world's definition of beauty.

Our other paper doll is a little plainer. Her name is Val U'Daughter, and we're not decorating her according to what she looks like on the outside, but by what's in her heart. God is showing us what beauty means as we study people like Esther, Lydia, Anna, and Ruth. We're writing down qualities like courage, patience, kindness, and love. The person that's emerging has a deep inner life—a life of true beauty. I hope we're all becoming more like her.

What I want to teach those girls, and what I want to learn myself, is that we *are* highly valued daughters of the King. Our beauty is not based on something we can do or even the looks or brains we've been given. It doesn't come in a bottle we can buy or pass away with age. Beauty, like joy, is so much deeper than that. It's based on who our Father is. And He doesn't change.

PRAYER AND REFLECTION:

My Father, my King, thank You for placing value on me and loving me and saying I am beautiful. Thank You that I am secure as Your child. My heart's desire is to have Jesus formed in me—in my inner being—so that I can reflect His beauty in the world.

Index of Scriptures

Old Testament

New Testament

Further Thoughts